MW00592655

HOW TO MANAGE
YOUR BOSS

For Sean Isaac Berkley,
who manages his ostensible boss
all too well

George E. Berkley

HOW TO
MANAGE
YOUR BOSS

A SPECTRUM BOOK

PRENTICE-HALL, INC.
Englewood Cliffs, New Jersey 07632

Library of Congress Cataloging in Publication Data

How to manage your boss.

"A Spectrum Book."
Bibliography: p.
Includes index.
1. Managing your boss. I. Title. II. Title: Manage
your boss.
HF5548.83.B47 1985   650.1'3   84-26356
ISBN 0-13-423641-6
ISBN 0-13-423633-5 (pbk.)

This book is available at a special discount when ordered
in bulk quantities. Contact Prentice-Hall, Inc., General-
Publishing Division, Special Sales, Englewood Cliffs, N.J. 07632.

10 9 8 7 6 5 4 3 2 1

Editorial/production supervision by Cyndy Lyle Rymer
Manufacturing buyer: Ann Armeny
Cover design by Hal Siegel

ISBN 0-13-423633-5 {PBK.}

ISBN 0-13-423641-6

Prentice-Hall International, (UK) Limited, *London*
Prentice-Hall of Australia Pty. Limited, *Sydney*
Prentice-Hall Canada Inc., *Toronto*
Prentice-Hall of India Private Limited, *New Delhi*
Prentice-Hall of Japan, Inc., *Tokyo*
Prentice-Hall of Southeast Asia Pte. Ltd., *Singapore*
Whitehall Books Limited, *Wellington, New Zealand*
Editora Prentice-Hall do Brasil Ltda., *Rio de Janeiro*
Prentice-Hall Hispanoamericana, S.A., *Mexico*

CONTENTS

ACKNOWLEDGMENTS

In the course of gathering material for this book I interviewed several people who had struck me as particularly adept at or knowledgeable about superior–subordinate relations. For the information and insight they provided me, I wish to thank Helen Clinton, Jon Chilingerian, Royal Cloyd, Robert Garretson, John Kotter, Donald Levitan, Lynne Lumsden, James Medeiros, and Marvin Siflinger. I am especially grateful to Robert Garretson, who responded to my written questions with a lengthy and perceptive letter.

I also deeply appreciate, as well as admire, Adelle Robinson for her uncanny ability to transform my handwritten scrawl into clean and error-proof copy. And I wish to thank my wife, Patricia, for sharing with me the birth pangs of this new and very different offspring.

THE BASIS
AND BENEFITS
OF BOSS
MANAGEMENT

1

MANAGING DOWN AND MANAGING UP

In 1974 an unusual book suddenly appeared on the best-seller lists. It was a voluminous (839 pages) and, for the time, costly ($17.95) introductory textbook setting forth the basic principles and practices of a particular profession. No one could remember ever having seen such a weighty and vocationally oriented work become one of the most sought-after books in the country. Yet its popularity proved to be no fluke, for the book remained on the best-seller lists for many months, comfortably lodged in the middle-to-upper range.

The book was Peter Drucker's *Management: Tasks, Responsibilities, Practices,* and its remarkable sales record attests not only to its writer's talents as a thinker and expounder but also to the widening appeal of his subject. Since then, other books on management have repeatedly cropped up on best-seller lists, and nearly all well-stocked book stores now display numerous titles relating to the topic. After decades of disinterest, a large portion of the book-buying public has become management-minded.

Many persons will find this new interest neither surprising nor strange. Are not present-day corporations influenced more by their managers than by their myriad and diffuse stockholders? Have not political scientists identified the bureaucracy, along with its professional managers, as the core of modern government? As Harvard professor Doris Kearns told me, "It's the bureau chiefs who really run the government." Are we not living in an age of organization, an age that enables and encourages those who manage organizations to become a primary force in shaping society?

Yes, management has emerged as a critical factor—some would say *the* critical factor—in modern life. Moreover, it is becoming more critical all the time. Our increasingly professionalized, fragmented, and complex world must place increasing emphasis on establishing goals and mobilizing people to work together to achieve them. Furthermore, nowadays prudent policy making all too often requires a depth and breadth of expertise that only those who implement policy can possess or tap. Consequently, legislators, boards of directors, and others whom we consider policy makers frequently must follow the lead of those whose ostensible function is merely to execute what the policy makers have supposedly decreed.

But if management and managers now play a pivotal role in modern life, the current preoccupation with the tools and techniques of their trade has created a tendency to overlook a few rather formidable facts. First, most of us who work in organizations cannot expect to become managers, at least in the sense in which this term is generally understood. The task of overseeing others presumes, obviously, that substantial numbers of these others will exist. But while many organizations, especially public ones, find themselves top-heavy these days with supervisory personnel of one kind or another, nonsupervisory personnel still outnumber them. There must always be more Indians than chiefs.

For those of the baby boom generation the outlook seems especially bleak. The baby boomers will form a bulge in the thirty-five to fifty-five-year-old sector of the work force for some time to come, and this is the age sector that supplies most of our managers. But their large number means that proportionately fewer baby boomers can look forward to managerial jobs. To make matters worse, many organizations have begun reducing their ranks of supervisory personnel to trim costs and give their rank and file employees more discretion.

All of this indicates that for the foreseeable future managerial posts will be in short supply. Those who have been busily learning how to manage subordinates may end up with no subordinates to manage. From this standpoint alone, they may find it advantageous to focus more attention on learning how to manage superiors instead.

But even the relatively few who do become managers may discover that they should have been concentrating more on handling relationships with superiors, for in moving upward they will come face to face with one important if often overlooked fact: *Nearly all managers have managers.* What's more, managers usually are more concerned with managing their superiors than they are with managing their subordinates.

"I have yet to sit down with a manager, whatever his level of job," writes Peter Drucker, "who was not primarily concerned with his upward relations and upward communications. Every president I know, be the company large or small, worries more about his relations with his board of directors than with his vice-presidents. Every vice-president feels his relations with the president are the real problem, and so on down to the first line supervisor, the production foreman or chief clerk, who is quite certain that he could get along with his men if only the 'boss' and the personnel department would let him alone." (Drucker, 1954)

Thus, the ambitious and able employee must expect to have to cope with bosses no matter how high he or she may rise. Unfortunately, most management books seem oblivious of this fact. Even Drucker, after calling attention to the overarching significance of relations with superiors, goes on to focus almost exclusively on how to manage subordinates.

But if you find the prospect of remaining a perpetual subordinate depressing, another factor should brighten the picture considerably. One can manage one's superiors as well as one's subordinates. One can manage up as well as down.

To begin with, the power of superiors even under the most authoritarian and arbitrary conditions has always been limited. For example, Frederick Law Olmstead found that slaveowners in the old South were continually confronted with effective resistance from their supposedly servile slaves. "That slaves . . . very frequently cannot be made to do their master's will, I have seen much evidence . . . ," he reported. "When they are directed to do anything for which they have a disinclination, they undertake it in such a way that the desired result is sure not to be accomplished."

Olmstead was not by any means trying to express sympathy for the slaveowners. Although better known as America's premier landscape architect—he designed New York City's Central Park and Boston's Public Garden—he was also an ardent abolitionist. Other observers, moreover, had noticed the same behavior. While slaveowners could abuse their slaves horribly, the latter still found ways of frustrating their masters' will.

If such was the power of slaves in the antebellum South, one can imagine the power of the average subordinate in the modern organization. Charles Frankel, a philosophy professor who once served as an assistant secretary of state, was struck by the interdependence between supervisor and supervisee. "In a bureaucracy that contains people with brains and consciences," he wrote, "an unspoken bargain binds the man at the top to his subordinates. If they are to be instruments of his will, he must to some extent be an instrument of theirs." (Frankel, 1968)

This condition is changing all the time, and for the most part, it is changing in favor of the subordinate. Many civil service regulations and union contracts have severely hampered the ability of superiors to discipline or dismiss subordinates. But even in situations free of such constraints, a new and more humanistic ethos has emerged to curb the discretionary power of superiors over those beneath them. Anyone who has studied organizations over the years has seen how treating people unfairly and inhumanely provokes much more unrest today than it did in times past. We should also remember that when superiors even discipline, let alone dismiss, an employee, they create a certain amount of trouble for themselves and cause their organizations a certain amount of expense. They also call attention to their own shortcomings, for every disciplinary action signals a managerial failure. Managers who must continually resort to such measures customarily find themselves facing career problems of their own.

Yet another aspect of the evolving superior–subordinate relationship is strengthening the subordinate's hand. When people work at the complex tasks of modern organizational life, they must continually exercise some degree of independence and initiative. Their superiors count on them to do more than they have specifically assigned them to do. Superiors who cannot rely on their employees for such extra effort usually do not stay superiors very long.

Organizational expert Rosemary Stewart relates how "one unpopular manager worked himself almost into the grave as his subordinates always did what he asked them to do and never did anything else." And she adds, "the more a manager needs the cooperation of his staff—and the more skilled and interrelated the work, the more he will need it—the less he can rely on formal authority to obtain it." (Stewart, 1972)

To sum up, the superior–subordinate relationship is becoming more of a two-way street with power and influence flowing in both directions. While subordinates rarely give orders to superiors, the amount of control they can exercise over their bosses' behavior is increasing all the time. Boss management, then, is not just an enticing but empty phrase; it is already a reality in numerous superior–subordinate relationships, and it is a potential reality in many others as well.

WHY SHOULD YOU MANAGE
YOUR BOSS?

Skillful subordinates—that is, subordinates skilled in handling their superiors—come in all shapes, sizes, and colorations. They can be liberals, like Walter Mondale, or conservatives, like Henry Kissinger. They can be callously cruel, as was Hitler's right-hand man, Martin Borman, or cheerfully good-hearted, as was Roosevelt's right-hand man, Harry Hopkins. They may use their skills primarily to advance their own selfish interests or primarily to advance the interests of their superiors. Most often, of course, they do both.

Some good subordinates remain subordinates forever; they shine only when serving a superior. But others use their abilities at managing bosses to become bosses themselves. In fact, most outstanding executives have throughout their careers demonstrated considerable dexterity in handling those above them. Dwight D. Eisenhower even managed to get along with the testy and temperamental Douglas MacArthur. Alfred P. Sloan, who built General Motors into the world's leading car maker, and Andrew Carnegie, who spearheaded the growth of the American steel industry, speak warmly, almost reverently, of their superiors in their autobiographies. Carnegie even named his first steel mill after his longtime boss and mentor Edgar Thompson.

This brings us to the first, and most obvious, benefit that boss management can bestow, namely, personal advancement. Although some authorities still like to cling to the cliché that good performance speaks for itself, nearly all those who have worked in or studied organizations of any kind believe differently. While competency in discharging one's duties is usually necessary for working one's way upward, it is rarely the sole ingredient or even the most important one in determining organizational success.

Professor John Kotter of the Harvard Business School points out some of the fallacies of the "good performance"

8

approach. In order for good performance even to be recognized, he says, five conditions must exist:

- some common conception of what the job is;
- some common agreement on the procedures or ways of doing it;
- some agreement as to how to measure performance;
- a designated person or device to do the measuring;
- a way of ensuring that this information reaches the boss.

As Kotter points out, all five conditions are seldom met in any one organization, public or private. Consequently, good performance remains an important but insufficient means for determining an employee's professional future.

In his landmark study *The General Manager,* Kotter notes how one of fifteen managers he studied was a talented and hard-working individual who "developed no strong relationships with upper management in his firm." Despite his ample gifts, the manager ended up receiving a transfer, which was widely perceived in his company as a demotion.

Columnist John "Dress for Success" Molloy tells of an in-house survey that a major corporation undertook on those who had been discharged from its employ. The corporation's president was startled to learn that the reason most often given for firing these people was their inability to get along with those they worked with or for. Inability to do the job was distinctly secondary in most cases.

The lesson to be drawn from these reports is apparent. Learn to manage your boss; *your present and future livelihood may depend on it.*

Another fact underscores the importance of boss management in realizing career expectations. Most successful top managers do not gain their positions by hopping from one company to another, as many people, including many business school professors, believe. Rather, successful managers tend to rise by moving from job to job *in different parts of the same company.* Even when they switch companies, they generally remain in the same industry. This means that your present boss's opinion of you can exercise an enormous influence over your future, since his or her voice will usually carry great weight within the same company or industry. Consequently, failure at managing a boss can overshadow the rest of your career and force you to look far afield for a fresh start.

Finally, an inability to handle superior–subordinate relationships can even affect your health. Researchers at the University of Washington have devised a scale to determine the amount of stress associated with various types of life experiences. Trouble with one's boss placed well up in the middle range of their stress scale. And they have found that the more stress an individual undergoes, the more vulnerable he or she becomes to numerous illnesses, including cancer.

But if failures in boss management can prove dangerous and even disastrous to your physical health as well as your professional future, successes can produce the opposite effect. Good boss management can make your present job much more pleasant while making future job prospects infinitely brighter. No one is likely to serve your interests better than a supportive boss. Such bosses may push you ahead of them or pull you up after them, depending on their, and your, predilections and plans. But a well-managed boss remains an enormous asset to anyone's career.

The case of John L. Raskob offers a telling illustration of what can happen. Raskob went to work as a typist for Pierre S. Du Pont when the latter was assistant treasurer at the already famous company that bore his family's name. When Du Pont moved up to treasurer, Raskob became assistant treasurer. When Du Pont became president, Raskob was promoted to treasurer, and when Du Pont took over the presidency of General Motors, in which the Du Pont Company then held a controlling interest, Raskob followed him, becoming chairman of GM's finance committee and its public spokesman.

Raskob was, by all accounts, a highly talented man. But not the least of those talents, and one that apparently loomed large in his success story, was his talent at managing Pierre Du Pont.

"UPWARD RELATIONS"

Skillful boss management can aid personal advancement in a different and less direct way. An example followed by the results of a research study will illustrate what I mean.

A group of consultants were once engaged to set up a human relations program in a small manufacturing company in New Hampshire. At the outset they ran into a yard superintendent whose supervisory style seemed the very antithesis of what they hoped to put into practice. This coarse fellow drove his employees mercilessly, cursed them loudly and frequently, and disciplined them severely. In short, he broke all the rules of good, enlightened management. Yet the team discovered, to its amazement and chagrin, that his employees not only had achieved high productivity but also showed a high degree of regard for their bumptious boss.

The confused consultants investigated and soon turned up some explanations. It seems that the yard workers considered their boss a "square shooter" who, if often ferocious, was nearly always fair. Moreover, he took a genuine interest in their welfare. He was always ready to advance them a few dollars until payday or render some other kind of help without patronizing them in any way.

But in probing further the consultants found a still more important factor at work: the superintendent's willingness to defend his employees' interests. During the previous ten years, the yard workers fondly recalled, he had twice stormed into the "big boss's" office to protest a decision he regarded as unfair to "his boys." When on one of these occasions the plant manager rejected his protest, the superintendent resigned on the spot, clamped his hat on his head, and strode out of the yard. To the great delight of the yard workers, the "big boss" ran after him, caught him as he was going out the gate, and agreed to the superintendent's demands.

The point that this incident illustrates is further borne out by a research study done at the Detroit Edison Company over thirty years ago. It found that company supervisors who used techniques that were considered good human relations practices developed no better morale and motivation in their employees than did supervisors who used less desirable methods. Further investigation soon showed why. The human relations–oriented managers were all too often viewed by their subordinates as ineffective in dealing with their own bosses.

This research study and the case of the yelling yard boss cast some light on an often overlooked aspect of successful management. *Managers cannot effectively manage their subordinates unless than can also manage their superiors.* They need support from above to obtain the resources and self-respect that their own employees require before they can or will do their best. There is nearly always a promotion or transfer to be approved, a rule to be changed or modified, a budget increase to be defended or a cut to be forestalled, an improvement in facilities to be obtained, or some other request or demand to be pressed, and the morale of their employees may ride on the outcome. Subordinates who perceive their superiors as unable to "produce" on such occasions quickly lose confidence in them. Such a perception then becomes self-fulfilling. Superiors viewed by their subordinates as ineffective will soon become just that.

Kotter's study of fifteen general managers spotlights the critical relationship between "managing up" and "managing down." These top-level managers were primarily concerned with maintaining good relations with their superiors, and they had good reasons for being so. "Getting the information, cooperation and support needed from bosses to do the job" and "being demanding with superiors without being perceived as uncooperative" were for them a constant and critical challenge. "Even in those cases where it was not a 'problem,' " says Kotter, "the task of 'managing up' was taken very seriously by the general managers. They all recognized that, to some degree, current job performance and future career success depended on it." And, he adds, "Such appears to be the case not only in other general management jobs, but in most other managerial jobs." (Kotter, 1982)

It is no wonder, then, that Peter Drucker thinks there is nothing inappropriate about the way managers worry more about relationships with their superiors than they do about relationships with subordinates. "Upward relations," he writes, "are properly a manager's first concern."

Another management expert, Kenneth A. Gold, approaches the issue from a still more positive perspective. When managers enjoy the confidence of their superiors, he writes, they "seem to pass this feeling of confidence on down the line to their subordinates. There is little doubt that this atmosphere of pride and confidence is infectious and creates a 'winning attitude' in the organization in the same way it does on a sports team." And, concludes Gold, "the significance of this dimension cannot be overestimated." (Gold, 1982)

HOW TO GET TWO PROMOTIONS AT ONCE

Improving one's managerial capabilities and advancing one's career by no means exhaust the benefits that adroit boss management can confer. There are other and less self-serving reasons for wanting to become proficient at this particular aspect of the managerial craft.

For one thing, good boss management can help not only you and your employees but your superior as well. In the long run at least, your superior's interests are likely to blend with your own. Such a convergence of interest does not, it is true, always characterize superior–subordinate relationships, and we will examine in some detail those situations where it does not later on. However, it does color and condition most such relationships much of the time. Many a subordinate has found that the best way to get promoted is to get his or her boss promoted. And many have succeeded in doing just that.

As already noted, good boss management can make a job not only more productive but also more pleasant. Often it yields an enriching personal relationship. To take a page from history, one might suppose Cardinal Richelieu to have had little respect for the oafish King Louis XIII, whom he managed so carefully and completely. Yet letters and other documents indicate that some genuine and mutual affection underlay their relationship. Catherine the Great's high regard for her adviser Potemkin is well-known. Queen Elizabeth became so attached to her right-hand man William Cecil that she visited him frequently when he lay dying, often feeding him herself. For years afterward she would sometimes burst into tears when recalling his memory.

But the examples of Richelieu, Potemkin, and Cecil point to a still more exciting and even an exalted motive for wishing to master the technique of boss management. Exercising it enables its more proficient practitioners to wield far more influence and accomplish much more than they could on their own. Richelieu, working with and through his monarch, gave France a unified and stable government. Cecil did much the same with Elizabeth. Potemkin helped Catherine the Great modernize Russia.

In more modern times Harry Hopkins originated and operated much of the New Deal before going on to become Roosevelt's chief emissary to Churchill and Stalin. And in 1953 a twenty-four-year-old law school graduate from the Midwest named Theodore Sorensen joined the staff of a newly elected senator from Massachusetts. Six years later Sorensen was writing the inaugural address for an incoming president. (John Kennedy's most famous phrase in that speech, "we must never negotiate from fear but we must never fear to negotiate," is regarded by Washington observers as pure Sorensen.)*

---

*It is interesting to speculate on what might have happened in history if two other valued subordinates had managed to live longer. John Rawlins, who served—and handled—Ulysses S. Grant as chief aide so well during the Civil War, died shortly after his superior moved into the White House. Had Rawlins lived, he might well have prevented the scandals that bedeviled Grant's presidency. He might even have succeeded in winning

Most of us, of course, cannot expect to become a Richelieu or a Potemkin or even a Harry Hopkins or a Theodore Sorensen. But skillful boss management can open up for all of us avenues to adventure and achievement that we might otherwise miss. It thus holds out the prospect of not just a more successful career but a richer and more rewarding life.

Congressional approval for Grant's ambitious scheme to annex Santa Domingo and turn it into a state for those recently freed southern slaves who were seeking a place of their own. (Grant's proposal, foolish as it may seem today, garnered considerable, though insufficient, Congressional support.)

Still more consequential, perhaps, was the assassination of Peter Stolypin, the prime minister of Czar Nicholas II, in 1911. Far more perceptive and pragmatic than his master, Stolypin might have steered Nicholas to a more moderate course and in so doing might have prevented the czar's ouster and eventual replacement by the Bolsheviks.

CHOOSING A BOSS WHO'S RIGHT FOR YOU

2

WHAT CHOICE DO YOU HAVE?

If your initial reaction to the title of this chapter is one of
skepticism or even scorn, I can certainly understand why.
Obviously, there is an element of exaggeration in the notion
of choosing a boss, just as there is in the whole concept of
managing one. But there is an element of truth in it as well.
For just as employees can and do exert considerable influence
over their bosses' behavior, so can they often exercise some
choice over what boss they will serve. And to the extent that
they can, they should certainly do so, for good boss management, like good employee management, best begins at the
selection stage.

But, you may protest, it's the job that's supposed to

count, not the boss. Furthermore, most of us most of the time have little choice about whom we will work for. We must take the boss who comes with the job we can get, or the one we already have, and go on from there.

These are, to be sure, valid points. The job itself will normally take precedence over the personality of the supervisor. In fact, one survey has suggested that one reason that women usually do not rise as fast or as far as men may be that they place more emphasis on the nature of the boss and less on the nature of the work than men do.* Furthermore, the jobs that most of us find desirable will probably be in short supply for many years to come. Such a situation scarcely seems likely to give many of us much chance to pick and choose among bosses.

Although such arguments are not without validity, there will nevertheless be times in your career when you will have some say over what superior you will serve. You may be desperately looking for work and feel as though you are ready to fling yourself off the nearest bridge in despair when you suddenly receive two fairly attractive job offers and have to choose between them. Or you may be working at a not-too-unpleasant job when you hear of an opening elsewhere and have to decide whether to apply for it. In situations such as these you will obviously want to take into account the boss that goes with the job. For good boss management becomes much easier when one has a good boss on whom to practice it.

But even when you lack any options and must merely accept the boss you have or will have, getting an idea of what to look for and what not to look for in a boss can help you understand, and deal more effectively with, the one fate has assigned you. As we shall see, some of the qualities you may think you abhor in a boss can actually prove advantageous,

*Margaret Hennig and Anne Jardin, in *The Managerial Woman,* also call attention to this difference between the sexes. They, however, attribute it in part to the experience men derive through sports and other activities in cooperating with those they may not necessarily like.

while some of the qualities you may think you desire in a boss can harm your career.

WHAT SHOULD YOU LOOK FOR?

In the course of interviewing successful subordinates—people who had worked their way upward despite often difficult bosses—I naturally asked each of them what qualities they found most desirable in a boss. While their answers differed, one characteristic was mentioned by virtually all of them: decisiveness.

To be sure, not all of them used this precise term. Some referred to "a willingness to take chances." But they all felt that a fearful, indecisive boss, one who hemmed and hawed in making a decision and who shied away from risks, was to be avoided at all costs.

When I mentioned this to Professor John Kotter, he was not at all surprised. Working with an indecisive boss, he said, is like "weaving your way through a mine field." One never knows when and where one is going to misstep, with damaging, if not disastrous results.

Think of it this way: Would you rather be sick and not know what was wrong, or would you rather know precisely what the illness was even though it was of a serious nature? If you cannot answer that question, just ask some people who have endured long bouts of medical uncertainty only to be finally told that they had a severe illness. Almost invariably they will tell you that the worst part occurred when they were in the dark as to what their malady was. Many will say that having it finally and definitively diagnosed came as something of a relief even when the diagnosis was not as favorable as they had hoped.

The reaction of many European leaders to Ronald Reagan offers another example. Many Washington observers expected Reagan to experience a lot of trouble negotiating with his European counterparts because his highly conservative views seemed so distant from theirs. Yet those European leaders, such as West Germany's Social Democratic premier Helmut Schmidt, who had dealt earlier with the moderately liberal Jimmy Carter found they preferred Reagan. For Reagan, at least, was fairly predictable; one knew what to expect. With the impulsive, inconsistent, and basically indecisive Carter, one could never be sure.

To be sure, indecisiveness and fearfulness are not identical traits, but they usually go hand in hand. Indecisive bosses will sometimes take a bold step, but often that is only because they have vacillated so long that the force of circumstance, or the force of their own frustration, has driven them to it. Such impulsive acts only add a further element of uncertainty to their practices and therefore to your position.

Indecisive bosses, as might be expected, frequently fear new ideas. But what really drives their subordinates to distraction is their frequent refusal to reject a new idea outright. Instead, the proposal and its proposer are kept in a state of suspended animation while the boss tries to make up his or her mind.

Bosses who dislike taking risks also dislike delegating. After all, they can never be certain how the work will turn out once they have surrendered day-to-day control. Many times such bosses will give you a challenging assignment and then, as their fears and misgivings mount, abruptly cancel it, rendering useless all the effort you have expended. Even when they allow you to continue with the project, they may destroy any joy or satisfaction you might have derived from doing it by requiring you to check with them every step of the way.

So one of the first things to look for in a boss is the ability to make hard decisions and take what might be called prudent risks. This does not in itself guarantee you a good boss, for those who have this ability may make poor decisions. They may also be hostile to new ideas and reluctant to delegate authority. And they may have other shortcomings as well. But they will almost always be better than those bosses who lack the ability to make decisions or to take risks. Remember that even when your boss makes decisions that you think are wrong, and makes them in a manner that you also regard as wrong, you can at least be reasonably sure most of the time of where you stand, so that you can decide how to proceed from there.

This brings us to another key aspect of the boss-picking process, namely, the boss's goals and objectives. What are they? More specifically, do they essentially match your own? Many people would put this criterion at the top of the list, and perhaps it does belong there. My only reason for relegating it to second place is that it does not seem to have played a major role in determining the boss preferences of most of those I interviewed. It may be that, as noted earlier, the goals and objectives of superior and subordinate naturally tend to converge more than they conflict. Bosses primarily want to impress their own bosses, and subordinates usually find it in their own interest to help them do so.

Nevertheless, conflicts and contradictions between the goals and objectives of superiors and those of subordinates do arise. Such conflicts are probably more common in the policy-oriented public sector than in the profit-oriented private sector, but they are by no means unknown in the latter. In checking out your future or present boss on this point, however, make sure you do not confuse goals and objectives with methods and procedures. Although the two categories often seem to shade into each other, one can and should try to demarcate them. A subordinate can usually adapt to and can sometimes even modify his or her boss's methods or procedures. Adapting to or changing a boss's goals and objectives is quite another matter.

Nearly all superior–subordinate relationships have been marked by virtually complete compatibility in terms of goals and objectives. To go back once again to history, Cecil and Elizabeth I fully agreed on the need to give England a strong, efficient government, to restore the national credit, to avoid war if at all possible, and to support the Reformation. They also shared a firm belief that work and pleasure were one and the same. The result was a relationship that greatly benefited both them and their country.

A third factor to take into account in assessing prospective or present bosses is the position they hold and the role they play within their organizations. Is the boss you are evaluating in a growing or a shrinking part of the company or agency? The answer can tell you a lot not only about your own prospects for getting ahead in the organization but about the nature of the boss as well. Smart supervisors tend to gravitate to the growing parts of their organizations. They avoid getting locked into dwindling or dead-end activities. Make sure you don't lock yourself in with a superior who has done so.

Managers on the move commonly construct networks of alliances. Has the boss you have in mind managed to do so? Remember that such networks can help you as well as your boss. Remember also that superiors who cannot do much for themselves cannot do much for their subordinates.

Making an inventory of your boss's network of friends and enemies will also give you an indication of his or her goals and objectives. You should keep in mind, however, that good managers customarily cultivate contacts with people whom they may not necessarily approve of or like. Therefore, the allies they have chosen do not automatically give a clue to their own values and goals. Enemies, on the other hand, can be much more revealing. If your boss has some, try to make sure that they are the right ones, that is, enemies that you would be likely to have if you were in your boss's position.

A fourth factor to be weighed in appraising bosses is the experience of others who have worked for them. If most of their employees tend to stay with them, that may be because they treat their employees quite well. However, it may also indicate that they have failed either to provide a springboard for their employees to advance or to attract employees capable of advancing. Probably, it indicates both situations. Bosses who experience little staff turnover are often good bosses but rarely are the best ones.

The best bosses are those whose subordinates regularly, though not rapidly, leave them to assume other, more challenging positions *within the same company or industry.* Such a pattern of employee movement tends to characterize bosses who have attracted good subordinates, developed their capabilities, and then helped them move ahead. Such bosses, it should be stressed, are serving not just their subordinates' interests but their own as well, for in "spinning off" their subordinates in this fashion they are seeding their organization or industry with people whom they can call on when they need information or assistance.

The worst bosses, on the other hand, are generally those who experience heavy staff turnover and whose employees, once they leave them, also leave the organization and often the industry as well. Such bosses can be fatal to your career.

In sizing up bosses with a view to managing them successfully, you should try to determine not only what they can do for you but what you can do for them. Boss management becomes much easier when you can offer something that they do not have and believe they can use.

This "something" can take the form of some technical expertise in, or specialized familiarity with, one or more areas that your boss regards as important. Franklin Roosevelt came from a rich, aristocratic family and grew up on a large estate in upstate New York. Harry Hopkins came from a modest midwestern family and had worked extensively among the urban poor. He could thus provide Roosevelt with information and insights that his superior lacked. Interestingly, when it came to choosing his own assistant at the Works Progress Administration, the gigantic relief agency he organized for the New Deal, the urban-oriented Hopkins chose a man who had worked extensively with the rural poor.

In many instances, a subordinate becomes invaluable to a superior by possessing personal qualities that balance or compensate for the superior's shortcomings. This is why so many of the best superior–subordinate relationships have been between people who seem like polar opposites. Richelieu was strong, clever, and industrious, while Louis XIII was weak, lazy, and none too bright. John Raskob was outgoing and, for a financier, ebullient, while Pierre Du Pont was rather formal and stiff. The quiet, reserved, and taciturn Cecil served an often dramatic and passionate queen. Potemkin possessed not only a knowledge of Russia that Catherine, being a German, did not have but also a daring imagination.

However, the more businesslike Catherine was able to bring his flights of fancy down to earth and put them to practical use.

With this in mind, you should look for a boss who is not too much like you. Though some common background is often helpful, and a common acceptance of certain basic goals may be indispensable, a degree of diversity can strengthen a superior–subordinate relationship.

Diversity can add other attractive dimensions to such a relationship. Royal Cloyd, for instance, was a young educational administrator in the Midwest when he heard about, and was urged to apply for, a position as director of adult programs for the American Unitarian Association. He journeyed to the association's headquarters in Boston and successfully passed the required interviews. He was not certain he wanted the position, however, until, standing on the steps of the association's Beacon Hill building and chatting with its old-line Boston president Frederick Eliot, he suddenly realized that, as he put it, "here was a man who knew about a whole level of life about which I knew nothing."

Cloyd took the position and served Eliot and Eliot's successors well before going on to become the founding executive secretary of the successful Boston Center for the Arts. He has never regretted responding to the lure and challenge of working for a boss whose personality and background differed so sharply from his own.

WHAT SHOULD YOU TRY TO AVOID?

While knowing what to value in a boss is important, knowing what not to value is of equal concern. Some personal qualities that might seem quite desirable in a social setting take on quite a different tone and texture when placed in a superior–subordinate context.

Foremost among such questionable qualities is an extreme desire to please. To be sure, most good bosses are basically decent people who treat their employees with respect.

But bosses who worry constantly about their employees' contentment are generally weak and insecure people who are really worrying about being liked. Ironically, in their eager efforts to make their employees happy they often end up exasperating them instead.

For one thing, such bosses may fail to promote or even protect your interests, for they are preoccupied with pleasing everyone else too. Your desired promotion, transfer, or new assignment may fall by the wayside if it runs into any real or imagined resistance from another quarter. In fact, you may often find it difficult to obtain the resources and authority you need for the task at hand. And should you become enmeshed in one of the many aggravating jurisdictional disputes that continually crop up in modern organizational life, don't count on such a boss for much help.

Even when such a boss deliberately tries to make you happy or to spare you pain, he or she can hurt you instead. Most management books talk a lot about the reluctance of employees to tell their employers unpleasant news. With the bosses I have been describing the problem may work the other way: the boss hesitates to tell you anything upsetting, which only causes you greater problems later on. Suppose, for example, that unbeknownst to you your job is in jeopardy. If you knew about it in time, you could make some attempt to put things to rights or at least look for another position while you are still employed. (Finding a job is almost always easier when you already have a job.) Unfortunately, your overly sympathetic boss dislikes telling you anything unpleasant, so you find out about it only when it is too late.

Think of it this way: Who is treating you more like an adult, and who is treating you more like a child—the boss who makes insistent demands on you without giving you much encouragement or sympathy, or the warm, friendly boss who's always eager to stroke your brow and hold your hand? One doesn't need to read any books on popular psychology to arrive at the answer.

This brings us to the problem of recognition for work well done, a sensitive subject in many superior–subordinate relationships. All of us want our efforts to be appreciated or at least acknowledged, for we cannot hope to move ahead until we have made our managers aware of what we are accomplishing. But this does not mean that we should need or even want frequent and fulsome praise. And, as it happens, many good managers praise little; some praise hardly at all. It was said of the master chef Escoffier, for instance, that when he looked at a subordinate's work and merely grunted, he was giving his highest accolade.

Although not quite as severe as Escoffier, General George C. Marshall also praised his subordinates sparingly. Yet many authorities regard Marshall, who served as Roosevelt's chief of staff in World War II and then became secretary of state under Truman, as perhaps the ablest public manager this country has ever produced. Dean Rusk, who worked for Marshall and who later became secretary of state himself, recalls only one instance when Marshall ever expressly acknowledged his efforts. Here is how he tells it:

> I had worked fourteen hours long into the morning and as I was leaving his office he said, "Mr. Rusk, you've earned your pay today." So I took that lesson from the greatest man I've ever known. If you have good people, it isn't necessary to compliment them. They know how good they are.

The lesson here for the wise and wary boss selector should be readily apparent. Fear not the boss who fails to give you frequent pats on the back. Remember that the best bosses are often the most demanding, and the best acknowledgment of your work they are likely to give you is to hand you tougher and more challenging assignments. That, you may find, is the best kind of recognition.

DO EXPERTS MAKE THE BEST MANAGERS?

Many a job seeker who has specialized in a particular line of work will look for a boss with a pronounced ability in the same specialty. Thus computer programmers, insurance agents, or detectives will want to work for computer programmers, insurance agents, or detectives whose professional proficiancy they admire or at least respect. They seek out such bosses with the understandable aim of improving their own skills and thereby advancing their careers.

Normally there is nothing wrong with such a strategy. In many cases it works well, for one may learn much in serving a master practitioner in one's own profession. But there are pitfalls in such a method of boss selection, and anyone concerned with boss management should take them into account.

To begin with, those who have become acknowledged experts in a particular line of work will in most cases have developed firm ideas about the nature of the work and how it should be done. They may respond coolly to, indeed may even feel threatened by, any suggestions you offer. They may insist that you do everything their way. After all, their procedures and practices have worked well for them, so why should they not work as well for you? Unfortunately, such an approach could be very harmful to your professional development.

A few years ago, the *New York Times* published a story about Jascha Heifetz, who had retired from the concert hall to devote himself to teaching. The *Times* expressed some puzzlement as to why the great violinist had turned out almost no outstanding pupils.

I put the problem to the late Joseph Berljawsky of Ottowa, who, while not a distinguished violinist, was considered the best violin teacher in Canada. Berljawsky quickly cleared up the mystery. "A great violinist will almost invariably tend to teach his pupils what worked best for him," he said, "but every violinist is different." He went on, "If I have a student who stands in a peculiar way or holds his bow in a particular way, then, so long as it does not seem to be interfering with his playing, I build my teaching around it. It's what works best for the student that counts."

Many master practitioners fail to follow this precept. In fact, they may be so insistent on having it done their way that they become loath to have it done by anyone else at all. They therefore end up trying to do everything, or at least everything that's important or challenging, themselves. Recognizing that they alone can utilize their own techniques most effectively, they dislike delegating meaningful responsibilities. As a result, their subordinates find themselves relegated to routine tasks. Even when such experts do delegate, they may supervise so closely and intervene so frequently that their subordinates experience little satisfaction in their work.

Contrast such a situation with that of working for Robert Moses, who splattered New York City with parks and laced it with parkways and other highways during the 1930s, 1940s, and 1950s. Moses had majored in English literature at Yale, and although he became an adroit public administrator, he knew little about the more technical aspects of his complex and costly undertakings. When he told his architects, engineers, lawyers, and finance men to do something, they frequently threw up their hands and replied that it couldn't be done. But Moses would brook no opposition, and his insistence would force them to find ways to do the seemingly impossible. Although many observers today rightly question the wisdom of many of Moses's projects, those who executed them developed skills and drew upon resources they never knew they possessed. Had Moses known more about their various fields, he might well have agreed with them when they branded his ambitious schemes as unattainable.

None of this means that you should rule out working for a superior who has shown superior accomplishment in your specialty. A young architect would have behaved strangely indeed in turning down a chance to work for the late Frank Lloyd Wright, and a budding psychoanalyst would certainly have missed out on a valuable experience in rejecting a job offer from Sigmund Freud. Nevertheless, a would-be subordinate in the process of selecting a superior should not automatically assign highest priority to the prospective boss's skills in the subordinate's own specialty. The benefits such bosses can confer may be negligible, while the problems they can cause may prove immense.

AGE, SEX, AND CHARISMA

There are three other factors that one should not overemphasize when choosing a boss. These factors are age, sex, and charisma.

In terms of age we commonly think of bosses as being older than ourselves. This seems not only proper but desirable, for older bosses can take a parental interest in their subordinates. In so doing, such a boss not only can make your work life more enjoyable but may also further your career.

But older bosses are not without disadvantages. They may prove quite resistant to change. They may look upon the initiatives and ideas of their subordinates as the immature whims of would-be whiz kids who think they know it all. "I know what works and what doesn't around here, for I possess the wisdom that only experience can confer," may be the older boss's implicit if not explicit response. "Just do things the proven way—my way—and everything will be all right."

The problem can become especially acute among older bosses who feel their own footing in the organization to be somewhat shaky. Such insecurity can make them doubly hostile to any suggestions from below.

One should also remember that some of the closest and most fruitful subordinate–superior relationships in history have been between older subordinates and younger bosses. William Cecil, Cardinal Richelieu, and Roosevelt's first assistant Louis Howe were all much older than their superiors. And in one case I know personally, a sixty-two-year-old executive assistant enjoyed an excellent relationship with a boss who had not turned forty.

However, this doesn't mean you should immediately try to trade in your older boss for a younger one. Young bosses, especially if they are appreciably younger than you, may feel awkward in having you as a subordinate. It is too much like giving orders to a mother or father (see "When Daughter

Becomes Boss.'') What's more, they may, even without any basis for doing so, regard you as something of a fuddy-duddy who could never adjust to, let alone institute, any new ideas.

This leaves bosses of the same age to be considered. Here too the situation contains both pluses and minuses. Such a

---

WHEN DAUGHTER BECOMES BOSS

While many subordinates have effectively and enjoyably served younger superiors, one growing trend in this direction has become a source of increasing tension and trouble. This trend is the tendency in recent years for older women to return to the work force once they have raised their children.

For the older woman such a step means surrendering her status as parent and homemaker. In many instances, it means giving up her status as a community leader as well. But adding to such aggravations is the fact that the middle-aged returnee may find herself working for a female boss young enough to be her daughter.

Such an age imbalance can create difficulties for both parties to the relationship. The older woman may become confused and resentful over such a role reversal. The younger woman may experience guilt and uncertainty over giving orders and criticism to a woman old enough to be her mother.

These problems were aired at a Simmons College symposium in the summer of 1984. One speaker, Betty Lou Marple, a middle-aged administrator at Harvard University, reported on an informal survey of two hundred such older women. She found them to have significantly different perceptions and expectations from younger women who enter the work force directly from college. One particular problem, she said, was the scarcity of older women supervisors and managers to serve as role models for the returnees.

"Women need to band together to empower themselves," concluded Marple. "Above all they need to talk about their differences and devise ways they can complement each other."

(The Boston Sunday Globe, August 19, 1984)

boss is more likely to think and act the way you do—to be on the same wavelength, so to speak. But a boss of similar age may feel more competitive toward you than an older or younger one.

Age, then, is a two-edged sword that can cut both ways in influencing superior–subordinate relationships. Consequently, it should not play a decisive role in determining whether the boss you are evaluating is one you want to work for. A boss's age in relation to your own will certainly have an impact on your relationship, but just what that impact will be will depend on the kinds of people you both are as well as the situation in which your relationship takes place. Unless you have specific needs or anxieties in this area, you would do well to discard any a priori notions of how old or how young a boss is best for you.*

Sex is another factor that should not receive undue emphasis in the boss selection or evaluation process. That it can influence managerial style has been well documented. The authors of that excellent book *The Managerial Woman* point out several ways in which women managers tend to differ from male ones. But these are only tendencies, and they are far from universal. Moreover, the differences between the two groups seem to be shrinking. So once again a priori notions should be shelved and choices should be made on an ad hoc basis.

Then there is the question of charisma. Charisma is an elusive quality that even the best dictionaries have trouble defining. One of them calls it "that special spiritual power or personal quality that gives an individual influence or authority over large numbers of people." Charismatic people possess a certain magnetic appeal that draws others to them.

Although charisma is more commonly associated with

---

*It is interesting to note that age seems to have had little bearing on overall managerial effectiveness. For example, anyone making up a list of Great Britain's greatest prime ministers would undoubtedly put the names of William Pitt and William Gladstone at or near the top. Yet Pitt became prime minister at the age of twenty-four, while Gladstone was still serving in that capacity at the age of eighty-four. And Winston Churchill was seventy when he became prime minister in England's "darkest hour."

political leaders, some managers possess it. And since charisma is an exciting quality, working for a charismatic boss is often an exciting experience. Such bosses can galvanize their subordinates into giving their utmost and in so doing force them to reach new levels of skill and efficiency. For these reasons, charisma in a boss can be a desirable quality.

But a charismatic boss can limit your growth as well. Awed by your superior's charisma, you may become blind to his or her errors and even misdeeds. Subordinates of charismatic bosses tend to go along uncritically with their bosses' plans and procedures without thinking things through for themselves. In so doing, they can produce a lot of trouble for themselves, their organization, and, when political leadership is involved, their country and the world. Autobiographical accounts of those who served such charismatic superiors as Adolf Hitler and Benito Mussolini bear ample witness to this fact.

To sum up, age, sex, professional or technical ability, compassion, and charisma do not in most cases deserve major consideration when it comes to choosing a boss. Certainly, they should be taken into account, and one or more of them could be crucial in a particular situation. But no hard and fast rules regarding their application can be laid down. The more you can free yourself from such concerns, the better boss manager you can become.

DIGGING A LITTLE DEEPER

In all likelihood, the foregoing will not exhaust the list of considerations you will want to bear in mind in evaluating a boss. One can easily think of several others, including a very important one that we will examine shortly. At this point, however, you may be wondering where you can discover and dig out all the information you would need to complete such a lengthy checklist.

Getting information about prospective bosses is not always easy, though it is often easier than it seems. There's a good chance that your would-be superior has occasionally had a write-up in the local newspaper. If he or she lives in one community while working in another, you might want to check the newspapers of both. A person may have remained a virtual nonentity in the city where he works but may have achieved a fair amount of prominence in the suburb where he resides.

In further pursuit of information you may wish to check professional and trade journals. There you may find not only write-ups about your boss but writings by him or her. Even the most action-oriented managers sometimes pause long enough to publish an article or letter in their field. And any piece of published writing that bears the boss's name should be taken seriously.

When Jimmy Carter had sewn up the Democratic presidential nomination in 1976, he began thinking about choosing a running mate. He invited four Democratic senators to spend a day each on his Georgia farm while he interviewed them for the position. After the process ended, he announced that Walter Mondale was his choice, saying that Mondale seemed the "best prepared." Later it was learned that Mondale was the only one of the four who had bothered to read Carter's autobiography *Why Not the Best?* before travling to Georgia.*

Probably the best sources of information about bosses are those who have worked for or with them. Try especially to seek out anyone who has ever held the position you are interested in. But remember that their reactions will reflect their own personal idiosyncrasies and preferences as much as those of the person they are describing. Your perceptions of and reactions to the boss in question might not be the same.

This brings us to a final factor that should figure in boss

---

*This is one example of Mondale's ability at boss management. A more general indicator is the fact that he acquired all the elective offices he has held through appointment. He was first named attorney general of Minnesota to fill a vacancy and was later appointed U.S. senator to fill another vacancy. He did manage to win reelection to both positions on his own, but his adroitness in handling political superiors, especially the late Senator Hubert Humphrey, helped win him the initial appointments.

assessment, and it may well be the most crucial one of all. You cannot hope to gain useful understanding of a present or potential superior without first understanding yourself. What are your goals, your values, and your needs? What pleases you in a boss, and what really rankles you? Of the things that rankle you, which are you prepared to accept and which are you not prepared to accept?

Only when you have answered these questions, and have answered them as truthfully and as fully as possible, can you hope to undertake successfully this initial and important step toward managing your boss.

HANDLING
THE EVERYDAY:
KNOWING,
LISTENING, AND
COMMUNICATING

3

Once on the job you are obviously in a position to learn much more about your boss. By all means do so. Knowledge is power, so Francis Bacon once said, and this holds as true for managing bosses as it does for managing nations. Of course, knowledge does not automatically translate into power. You can amass a mountain of data about someone, but if you don't interpret it correctly and utilize it intelligently, the data will be worthless. Nevertheless, knowledge does provide the basis for exercising influence in human relations, as in almost everything else.

What kinds of things should you try to find out? Just about everything. What is your boss's geographic, educational, professional, even ethnic and religious background? How long has he been with the company, and in what capacities has he served? What about work habits? Is she, for example, a "morning person" or an "afternoon person"? What about career goals, opinions of others in the organization, political preferences? Answers to these and countless other questions are all appropriate for your files. (Not that you need to keep an actual dossier on your boss. Usually, just storing the information in the back of your mind will suffice.)

Do not neglect the personal or the trivial. If your boss has a bad back or a bad tennis backhand, a handicapped child or a high handicap in golf, you should know about it. Just about everyone who studies human interactions at work comes away convinced that the seemingly unimportant or irrelevant can be very important and very relevant.

In pursuing your quest for information you should range not only wide but deep. For example, it is not enough to know that your boss has three children, two girls and a boy. You should also find out whether any or all of these children are a source of perpetual pleasure and pride, a source of continual embarrassment and mortification, or a source of any concern at all.

Be careful not to leap to conclusions based on your initial findings. If your boss has an M.B.A. from Dartmouth, you may think she is proud of having earned such a degree from such a prestigious Ivy League school. But it could be that she really wanted an M.B.A. from Harvard and feels annoyed about or even ashamed of having been rejected by that "West Point of American capitalism." Conversely, if your boss never went to college, you may feel she is probably disdainful or jealous of your own M.B.A. from Harvard. Yet it could be that your boss enjoys having a Harvard M.B.A. as a subordinate and likes to boast about it.

Although apparently minor factors can play major roles in shaping a superior–subordinate relationship, some aspects of your boss can still be earmarked in advance as deserving special attention. One in particular stands out. The English writer G. K. Chesterton perhaps put it best.

> There are some people—and I am one of them—who think that the most practical and important thing about a man is still his view of the universe. We think that for

a landlady considering a lodger it is important to know his income, but still more important to know his philosophy. We think that for a general about to fight an enemy it is important to know the enemy's numbers, but still more important to know the enemy's philosophy. (Chesterton, 1904)

Chesterton carved out his niche in history as a novelist and literary essayist; he certainly never posed as an expert in organizational relationships. Yet anyone wishing to manage a boss, or anyone else for that matter, would do well to heed these words.

Discovering the facts about your boss and discerning the truths behind them will, of course, be much easier when you are on the job. Simply observing her in action will tell you much. You will also have access to many other sources of information as well.

The most obvious one is your boss's official biography. It's almost certain to be around somewhere in the form of a résumé or press release. You should examine it carefully, taking note not only of what it says but of what it does not say. If, for instance, it makes only the slightest reference or no reference at all to educational background or family or outside activities, this may tell you something worth knowing about the person you are working for. (Such omissions could, however, reflect company attitudes and policies or other factors. Again, don't be too hasty in drawing conclusions.)

A person's office can be revealing. Is the furniture old-fashioned or modern? Is it dominated by a desk, or does it have a couch, lounge chairs, and other facilities for informal seating? What pictures are on the wall? What mementos are on the desk?

You will naturally want to talk with others who work for or with your superior. In sounding them out, however, it is usually best to avoid asking point-blank questions such as "What is so-and-so really like?" Rather, ask about a particular issue or problem, or simply report an incident involving your boss and then await the response. Eventually you should find out much of what you want to know.

You may also want to carry this indirect approach still

further, posing your questions in such a way that you are
really asking your sources about themselves. For example, in
questioning the boss's secretary, you may want to ask when
she began working for the boss, what if any difficulties she
experienced, and so on. It is important not to treat people
simply as reservoirs of information about someone else but
as individuals in their own right. Don't forget that you normally want to build good relationships with them as well, and
manifesting interest in them as individuals is crucial to such
relationships.

Spouses can be especially sensitive to any suggestion that
they are being viewed as mere appendages to their mates.
Should you have occasion to talk at any length with your
boss's spouse, respond to him as you would to any interesting
person you might meet. This does not, of course, mean that
you must pretend to find a spouse more interesting than he
is; for you, such a person will probably be most interesting
in representing a major decision, as well as constituting a major factor, in your boss's life.

One final note on this point: While most people respond
favorably to any interest shown in them as individuals, you
cannot usually build good relationships on the basis of interviewing alone. In fact, people often become a bit suspi-
cious of those who merely ask questions and volunteer no
information about themselves. So don't be afraid to interject
yourself, moderately and modestly to be sure, into the conversation. If your boss's wife likes to go to the theater, mention the plays and performers you have seen recently and say
how you felt about them. Just make sure you also find out
her theatrical likes and dislikes too. And if in the process you
also learn something of her husband's preferences in this regard, so much the better.

At this point you may be wondering whether all this
information is really necessary or even especially useful, when
so much of it seems to bear so little relationship to the work
you and your boss are doing. Let me provide just a few examples of how it can serve to strengthen your relationship to
your superior.

Some applications are quite apparent. A boss with a

handicapped child will obviously be more responsive to hiring handicapped people, establishing facilities for the handicapped, and so on. If you are a plant manager or a regional office manager and your boss is coming for a visit, you would probably do well to make sure that your own building reflects some sensitivity to such concerns. (Of course, you should want to do this anyway.)

If your boss also has a bad back, then in making hotel arrangements for her visit you will want to see that her bed is equipped with a bed board. Naturally, you would like her to know about your thoughtfulness, but try to have someone else, possibly the hotel staff, tell her about your good deed.

Other uses of information about your boss may be less obvious. Some Italian Americans, for example, have become disturbed about all the publicity the Mafia has received in recent years. They feel it reflects unfavorably on all Italian Americans, the vast majority of whom have never even met a Mafioso. If your boss is of Italian descent, you might want to think twice before making indiscriminate use of the term, such as applying it jokingly to the operations of a rival organization.

Suppose that your boss likes football. Then how his favorite team fares on the weekend could well affect his mood on Monday. (This is especially likely if he also bets on the game.) Glancing at the weekend football results, with perhaps a special glance at how his favorite team made out, may make you better prepared to deal with him on Monday morning.

People who like football—and many male executives do—usually enjoy watching any good professional or college game, not just one involving their favorite team. One company president couldn't understand why he was usually so irritable and impatient at his Tuesday staff meetings. Eventually he realized that "Monday Night Football" was the reason. He watched the televised games faithfully, and while lying in bed afterward he would go over the plays in his mind. This interfered with his rest, leaving him tired and out of sorts the next day. Once he discovered the cause of his Tuesday morning grumpiness, he switched the staff meetings to

Thursday. A smart and informed subordinate might already have noted what was happening and thereby have helped him to make the welcome change earlier.

Superiors often appreciate the value of a subordinate who knows them well. During the American Revolution, George Washington was asked what qualifications he considered most important in choosing military aides. "They ought," Washington replied, "to possess the Soul of the General; and from a *single* Idea given to them, to convey his meaning in the clearest and fullest manner."

As it happens, a young captain named Alexander Hamilton managed to meet Washington's criterion best. Hamilton never became as close to Washington as some of the general's other aides. How could he, since he was the ambitious, commercially-minded, urban-oriented son, and an illegitimate son at that, of a drifting Scottish peddler, while his boss was a wealthy, cultivated, and somewhat aristocratic planter? But, as historian Broadus Mitchell has observed, "Hamilton came to understand Washington's intentions so well that he could anticipate them in a given instance and express them in language such as the commander-in-chief would use." (Broadus, 1976) There is no question that Hamilton was a man of extraordinary talents; but not the least of these talents, and the one that eventually helped make him the most influential figure in the first federal government, was the ability to understand and thereby to manage his boss.

ACTIVE LISTENING

Barbara Walters tells of a young woman attending a cocktail party who, when anyone asked her how she was, would promptly answer, "I'm dying." Her questioners would then respond with phrases such as "That's good" or "You look great."

Alas, cocktail parties are not the only places where little real listening takes place these days. As a nation, we seem to have plugged up our ears. We may allow other people to talk, but much of the time we only pretend to listen to what they are saying. Or we fade in and out, catching an idea or phrase here and there while waiting for them to finish so that we can have our say. Frequently we are so busy framing our answer to the first thing they said that we fail to hear anything that followed. No wonder psychologists are constantly reminding us that the key to successful relations with our family members and friends lies in listening, really listening, to what they are saying.

The same exhortation holds true for the world of work. "Listening is really a matter of critical importance in the business world," says Gordon Crosby, president of U.S. Life. "Understanding cannot be obtained from simply reading or speaking. Others have to be able to communicate with you." (Schoenberg, 1978)

The ability to listen is especially important to subordinates, for bosses expect to give orders or at least directions, and they expect their employees to follow them. No subordinate can hope to avoid conflict with, let alone exercise influence over, a boss unless he is prepared to listen carefully to everything the boss has to say.

Good listening involves much more than simply remaining quiet while your boss is speaking. You must learn to be what the psychologists call an "active listener." This means hearing not just what is being said but what is being implied. It means taking careful note of what is being emphasized and what is being omitted. And it means being able to summarize and respond intelligently to what you have heard.

Perhaps the greatest impediment to active listening is a feeling of insecurity. As Barbara Walters puts it, "Undoubtedly, inner confidence is the key to making genuine contact with another person. Nervous people are too involved with their own alarm bells and flashing signals." Unfortunately, many subordinates fall into this category. They are so busy looking for signs of approval or disapproval in their boss's words, and thinking of explanations or suggestions to defend themselves or prove their worth, that they often miss the real thrust of what is being told them.

Few people can rid themselves of their insecurities by a mere act of will. But if they can recognize such feelings and the role they play in preventing active listening, they can bring them under some form of control.

The most obvious step, though certainly not the easiest, is to forget about yourself and concentrate as completely as you can on what your boss is saying. Make sure you are looking at her, creating some eye contact without prolonged staring. When she is finished, don't immediately rush in with a response. A slight pause will signal that you have listened carefully and are now letting her words sink in. When you do respond, do so in a way that indicates how well you have listened. You might ask a question or two in seeking clarification or amplification on one or more matters that she has raised, or you might merely summarize in a sentence or two, or even a word or two, what she has said. Remember that bosses really appreciate subordinates who never have to be told anything twice. Make sure your boss knows that you intend to get it right the first time.

You may often find it helpful when your boss is talking to you to make written notes. These notes need not and should not be elaborate, for bosses do not want to be held up while you are writing. Furthermore, writing down one idea too fully may keep you from taking in the idea that follows it. But jotting down a quick note or two when the boss is telling you something can be most useful. For one thing, it will force you to be an active listener. For another, it signals your boss that you are taking her message seriously.

To facilitate such note taking you should develop a shorthand of your own with a set of abbreviations for the words most commonly used in your work. You may also want to keep a small note pad handy in your pocket or purse. (Martin Borman, at meetings with *Der Fuehrer,* scribbled notes on his cuff.) If the instructions your boss has given you are quite detailed, you may find it useful to write up your notes in more expanded form once you are by yourself.

If your boss has given you an assignment that cannot be completed right away, it may be wise to give him some fairly quick feedback on the steps you are taking to carry it out. This will reassure him that you have not forgotten it. It will also give him an opportunity to amplify, modify, or even cancel the task. New developments or simply second thoughts may have caused him to want to alter his original instructions, and, in the press of daily decision making and problem solving, he may have forgotten to tell you about it. Such things happen all the time.

When listening to your boss, stay alert for special code words, speech inflections, and the like. These cues may reveal more about what is going on in her mind than her sentences themselves. Also be aware of any body language she may be using. Body language is a field of developing importance, and anyone who wants to work successfully in organizations would do well to learn some of its basic principles.

You should be an active listener, not just when your boss is talking to you but when he is talking to others, and not just when he is busily at work but when he is relaxing. Harry Hopkins, for example, always remained alert to any expression of his boss's wishes and then, if it was possible and suitable, translated them into reality. Once while attending a dinner party with Roosevelt when the latter was governor of New York, he heard his boss mention casually to another guest what a great thing it would be to offer young men from the slums a chance to work in the fresh air helping preserve the state's forests. Hopkins sprang into action the following day and soon 10,000 impoverished city youths were working in upstate woodlands. (This program was the forerunner of the Civilian Conservation Corps, which Roosevelt launched when he became president.)

Active listening, however, should not always spur you to speedy and forceful action every time your boss expresses a whim. Some of his expressed yearnings will probably be too trivial to bother with. Others may be too dangerous. Often a boss will blurt out a desire for something that, on reflection, he would quickly think better of. Occasionally, even express commands to do something are best left unacted upon for your boss's good as well as your own.

John Ehrlichman, one of Richard Nixon's closest aides, has described how his frequently frustrated boss would occasionally issue the most outrageous orders. Executing these orders would not only have involved improprieties as great as, if not greater than, those which brought on the Watergate scandals but, being more overt, would have immediately triggered cries of outrage in Congress and the press. The members of Nixon's staff, however, had learned to nod their heads deferentially when they received such instructions and then quietly to forget them. They had come to realize that their testy boss was just letting off steam and never really meant his off-the-cuff—and off-the-wall—commands to be carried out.

SPEAKING CONCISELY AND WRITING CLEARLY

Boss management mandates not only that you listen carefully to your boss but that you induce your boss to listen carefully to you. This latter task is usually much more difficult, since it seems less natural to the superior–subordinate relationship. After all, it's the boss who's supposed to give the orders; it's the employee who's supposed to receive them. This stereotype tends to cast the superior's relationship to the subordinate in an "I talk/you listen" mold. Many bosses find it hard to break away from such a pattern; some find it next to impossible.

Another element that impairs the upward communication process lies in the nature of managerial work itself. It is, for one thing, continually ongoing. In other professions there are terminal points. The building is completed, the patient is cured, the case is settled. Such distinct points of closure do not occur in management, at least not in the same way. Projects may be completed and problems may be resolved, but as long as the manager's organizational unit continues to operate, the manager's work continues as well.

Managerial work is also unlike other professions in being open-ended. Ordinarily there is only so much time that an architect, doctor, or lawyer can usefully spend designing a building, treating a patient, or fighting a case. But a manager invariably has more to do than she possibly can. Delegation, which is the very heart of managment, implies that a manager cannot do it all. And no matter how smoothly and efficiently an organization or one of its units may function, there are always opportunities to be explored and improvements to be made.

Thus, those who manage inevitably find their days too short. (If they don't, then they are probably bad managers.) This is why books on management devote so much attention to the problem of managing time. Time is often a manager's greatest yet scarcest resource, and managers of any degree of ability guard it carefully.

With this in mind, the first thing a subordinate must learn in order to communicate well with a superior is brevity. Shakespeare called brevity the soul of wit; it is the soul of good boss management as well.

Gordon Crosby, the U.S. Life president cited earlier, is also a teacher of management, and one thing he requires his students to master is the art of preparing and delivering what he calls an "elevator speech." This, says Crosby, is "the all-encompassing, action-producing set of ideas and facts that you pronounce while on the elevator with the big boss for just one minute." (Schoenberg, 1978)

An elevator speech can come in handy in many other situations besides elevators. Sometimes the only way you can get your superior's ear is to accompany him down the corridor from one office to another. You should know how to make maximum use of such an opportunity.

Being brief does not mean jamming a lot of information into a rapid-fire monologue. It means being selective and direct. One can do this and still be relaxed and informal. In his book on general managers, John Kotter transcribes a conversation between a manager and his subordinate that took place as the manager was standing in the hall ready to turn into his office. In an easygoing manner the pair exchanged much useful information covering a wide variety of topics. Yet the entire exchange lasted only two minutes.

Not all your contacts with your immediate superior will be limited to brief encounters in elevators and corridors. But even in more scheduled and drawn-out discussions you should guard against rambling, prolixity, and beating about the bush. Such approaches rarely win a boss's favor.

When it comes to written communication the same basic stipulations apply. While conciseness and clarity should govern all your writing, they should particularly characterize the writing you submit to a superior. Some bosses require that memos addressed to them be no longer than one page. Even if your boss doesn't have such a rule, you should try to follow it whenever possible. Naturally there will be times when you will want or need to send her lengthier material. The situation may require a detailed report, and your boss may be expecting one. Also, presenting an in-depth analysis demonstrates that you have done some serious work on the project and thus helps establish your authority to speak on it. But even when submitting such a document you may do well to place on top of it a one-page summary of its contents or list of highlights. Such a summary page will enable your boss to get quickly to the gist of what you have to say. She can then decide how much of the rest she needs to read—or whether she needs to read any of it. In many instances, the summary page itself may suffice.

Bosses differ in the extent to which they prefer written to oral communication. Most of them are action-oriented, outgoing people who lean toward the oral form. Such person-to-person contact permits speedy coverage of a range of matters and provides immediate feedback as well. It also puts communication on a more natural and human level. But there are two very different kinds of bosses who gravitate toward the written form.

One group consists of procrastinators and risk avoiders who like everything in writing so that they can delay making a decision and cover themselves once they do make it. The other group is made up mostly of top-level managers who usually lack the time to process all the information they must obtain unless this information is in written form. Robert MacNamara, who has served as president of Ford Motor Company, secretary of defense, and president of the World

Bank, always preferred written briefings to oral ones. As he said on one occasion, "I can read faster than they can talk."

For various reasons having to do with accountability, written communication plays a more important role in government than in business. Consequently, many public officials owe a good deal of their success to their ability to summarize a situation and articulate its various aspects succinctly. Several of the able public-sector subordinates cited earlier, such as Alexander Hamilton, George C. Marshall, Dean Rusk, and Dwight Eisenhower, all possessed this talent, and it helped them immeasurably in winning their superiors' favor. But facility with the written word can advance a business career as well. There will always be times when you will want or need to communicate with your boss in writing, for only when ideas and information are put in this form can they be developed extensively and circulated widely.

How does one develop such a skill? Courses in business writing as well as books on style can help. Among the latter I especially recommend *The Elements of Style* by William Strunk, Jr., and E. B. White. One good practice for improving all kinds of prose, but especially organizational

PEN OVER SWORD

Although writing ability scarcely seems an indispensable ingredient for military success, it has advanced the career of many an officer in the U.S. Army. Aside from Alexander Hamilton, whose talent with the pen helped him become General Washington's chief military aide, literary ability also figured prominently in the rise of Generals George C. Marshall and Dwight D. Eisenhower. It was Marshall's valued assistance to General John Pershing in helping the latter write his memoirs that made him stand out in his superior's eyes. Marshall, in turn, leaned heavily on Eisenhower, then a young captain, for help with the project. As Hamilton himself once noted, no one should ever underestimate the "power of statement."

prose, is to read aloud what you have written. If it sounds good, it will almost certainly read well. And if what you have written is of more than routine importance, you might want to have a colleague or friend go over it before sending it to your superior.

Keep one thing firmly in mind. Good prose probably reflects not so much an ability to write as an ability to think. It has been truly said that there are no clear writers, only clear thinkers. Therefore, make sure you have thought the matter through and arranged your material clearly and coherently before you sit down at your typewriter or word processor.

COMMUNICATING WITH NUMBERS

Words are not the only medium of expression in organizations. Figures also play a large role in conveying information, and they can be particularly helpful in communicating with bosses. Numbers have an aura of cool objectivity that superiors find appealing. Furthermore, it is always more effective to show people something than to tell them something, and this is especially true when a subordinate is trying to get an idea across to a superior. Numbers enable us to do this. Finally, such symbols meet the need for brevity and clarity, since a number or two can often summarize an entire page of written material.

Numerical information can be made still clearer and more compelling through the use of charts and graphs. A line on a graph can reveal what would otherwise take a long list of figures or pages of prose to explain. Charts and graphs are particularly effective in depicting changes or exceptions. If there has been a sudden drop-off in sales, a graph will instantly show it. If one department is producing much more, or much less, than the others, a bar chart will quickly and dramatically pinpoint that fact.

For reasons such as these, many executives respond well to information presented in this form. Franklin Roosevelt loved charts, and his aides soon learned how to use them to drive home a point. President Reagan, it appears, is equally susceptible to such techniques. When Budget Director David Stockman found he could not get his boss to appreciate the gravity of the government's fiscal crisis, he presented the possible scenarios in graphic form. Only then did his incurably optimistic boss start to make some of the hard choices that the situation demanded.

If you have graduated from a decent business school or

WHAT'S THE PERCENTAGE?

One of the most effective yet easiest ways of conveying the import of numerical data is through the use of percentages. To tell your boss that sales of item X increased by 142 last month forces him to recall the previous month's sales record for item X and assess the significance. To say that sales of item X were up 18 percent last month gives him an immediate grasp of what has occurred.

The simplest way of translating a numerical change into a percentage is to divide the new figure by the old or base figure, subtract 1 from the result, and then muliply by 100. For example, if sales increased from 50 to 100, compute the percentage change as follows:

$$\frac{100}{50} - 1 \times 100 = 100\%$$

If sales decreased from 100 to 50, then the same formula provides the following equation:

$$\frac{50}{100} - 1 \times 100 = -50\%$$

Note that while the change in both instances is 50, in percentage terms it represents 100 in the first instance and 50 in the second. This is because the base figure or denominator has changed. Fifty represents 100 percent of 50 but only 50 percent of 100.

have had a course in basic statistics, you should have no trouble compiling appropriate figures and drawing graphs and charts to illustrate them. If you lack such a background, you may want to glance at a statistics book. Usually, the first chapter or two will provide enough instruction to enable you to make use of such material on a basic level. (See the accompanying box for a brief rundown on one of these techniques.)

One final caveat: Don't overutilize such devices. It is not usually necessary to prepare detailed statistical data or elaborate charts and graphs to illustrate everyday information. If you do, your boss may start to wonder how wisely you are using your time. Although an appropriate statistic or two, and perhaps a simple graph, can come in handy to back up even the most routine and casual report, more complex data and more complete diagrams are best saved for special occasions. Artfully prepared and presented at such times, they can help you sell not only your ideas but yourself as well.

SOME FINE POINTS OF COMMUNICATION

Here are a few additional guidelines to keep in mind when communicating with your boss.

Don't be too eager to offer your opinions. If you wish to get a point across, marshal the facts that support your point and try to present them in such a way that the point becomes obvious. If the suggestion or idea you wish to advance is not taken up by your listener, you may wish to offer it indirectly by saying, "With all this in mind, I wonder if it might be useful to try . . ." or "Do you think we should consider . . . ?" Try as much as possible to let the idea emanate from the boss rather than yourself.

The same guideline should generally govern your response even when your boss asks you directly for your opinion about some matter. Note briefly the pros and cons of the issue, and then offer your opinion in such a way as to indicate that you would be happy to change it should other relevant facts come to light. Be especially careful not to reject out of hand any proposal he mentions, for even if he presents it as coming from someone else, he probably has seen some merit in it or he would not have bothered seeking your reaction. First try to find some merit in the idea, and only then present whatever objections you may have. These objections can be presented in the form of questions, such as "Do you think we could make this change without disrupting our production schedule too much?" or in the form of objections others are likely to make, such as "The personnel office might raise the roof on this." If you can at the same time indicate that your objections are based on data not available to him, so much the better. Thus, you might say, "I know that Personnel is getting very touchy on this point, for I was just talking to so-and-so at lunch today and she told me . . ."

Keep your eyes peeled for any item in the newspapers, trade journals, and other publications that might interest your boss. If you suspect that she has not seen it, clip it or photocopy it and send it along. If the item is a long one, you may want to underline the most pertinent passages. If it's something you heard on radio or television, you may want to type up a short summary and send it to her.

Respect for your boss's time need not prevent you from passing along information of less than major importance. Bosses often welcome brief human interest items from the workplace, especially if they strike a positive note. They often appreciate humorous items as well. In fact, humor and even abbreviated discussions of nonwork subjects such as sports frequently crop up in superior–subordinate interchanges. Professor Kotter has found such digressions helpful in serving "as effective tools for building relationships and maintaining them under stressful conditions." Just make sure to keep any such digressions that you originate short.

Finally, there is the story of Project Gorilla. It illustrates some of the points touched on in this chapter and, more importantly, offers an example of a smart subordinate in action.

The story concerns a West Coast manager who likes his

independence but realizes that it can be secured only through shrewd boss management. Every year this manager must journey to his company's East Coast headquarters to obtain the necessary approvals, funding, and so on for his operations. For the event he prepares a rather elaborate presentation complete with charts, graphs, demonstrations, and the like. One year, faced with obtaining consent for a more ambitious undertaking than usual, he put together such a graphic and complete presentation that when it ended, his boss slapped his knee and exclaimed, "Jim [not his real name], even a gorilla could understand what you have in mind."

Once he had obtained the go-ahead, Jim decided to call the new undertaking Project Gorilla. By allowing his boss to name it, Jim had involved him in the project. Returning to the West Coast, Jim contacted the local zoo and got a quantity of bumper stickers bearing the question "Have you hugged a gorilla today?" Soon all those associated with the operation had bumper stickers on their office walls as well as on their cars. In this breezy, good-humored manner, Project Gorilla was launched. Like most of this manager's undertakings, it became a solid success.

HANDLING THE EVERYDAY: SPECIFIC SUGGESTIONS

4

SOLVE YOUR OWN PROBLEMS

In the preceding chapter we saw how the open-ended and ongoing nature of managerial work tends to make time a manager's scarcest resource. Probably nothing eats away at this more voraciously than employees who cannot solve their own problems. Although some managers, almost always inferior ones, like to have their employees continually come to them with problems, most managers find that a heavy burden. As one of Professor Kotter's managers expressed it, "It never ceases to amaze me how many people want to see me and how many different problems they come up with. We could schedule meetings all day and all night if we didn't try to control it."

Having to deal with their subordinates' problems deprives them not only of time but frequently of influence as well. Most subordinates tend to exaggerate the power and authority of their boss. It is usually more limited than it appears. And almost every time it is used, it is to some degree used up. You may not think you are asking for very much when you ask your boss, say, to call Personnel or Production to straighten out a minor matter. But suppose she is already trying to get their cooperation or assistance on something else. In fulfilling your request, she tends to weaken her position regarding the more important (to her) matter she has pending, for one can only ask so much of others. And even if she has no request pending, she knows that fulfilling your request today will make it just a bit more difficult to fulfill a similar request for herself or someone else tomorrow.

In pushing problems onto your boss, you damage not only his ability to do his job but your ability to do yours. For one thing, you will probably fail to develop the skill and contacts you need to work effectively. For another, you will create a poor image of yourself in his eyes. Nothing can be more fatal to your career than a reputation for being unable to handle the normal vicissitudes of organizational life, even when they are not directly related to your work.

"We hired a bright 28-year-old portfolio manager from a bank in Wisconsin," relates U.S. Life Chairman Gordon Crosby, "and within three weeks, maybe four, he had sold his home in Madison, purchased a new home in Summit, New Jersey, and was on the job. We had another situation, an internal transfer, where it took the man almost nine months to make the move." Adds Crosby, "Now that told us something." (Schoenberg, 1978)

Generally speaking, you can do both yourself and your boss a great favor by keeping problems away from her door. You may sometimes feel a desire to let her know about them just to impress her with the difficulties of your position. For the most part, you will do well to resist such a temptation. Bosses believe they have problems enough of their own, and they may not be as sympathetic to your plight as you might wish. On the other hand, most bosses appreciate employees who rarely seem overwhelmed by their tasks.

One kind of problem that is growing in frequency and that bosses particularly dislike dealing with is jurisdictional disputes. When the conflict involves two parties within their own area of authority it becomes especially touchy and troublesome. For if the boss favors one side, he risks antagonizing and alienating the other side, while if he seeks a straight compromise by splitting the dispute down the middle, so to speak, he may end up having to accept a woefully imperfect solution. So in trying to keep problems away from your boss, try especially hard to do so when they involve ju-

---

GRANT'S GIFT

In 1856 former U.S. Army captain Ulysses S. Grant was selling firewood on the streets of St. Louis in yet another failing attempt to feed his family. Less than eight years later he had become the second most powerful man in the nation, commanding a war machine of a size and scope unknown since the days of Napoleon. Behind Grant's remarkable rise lies a remarkable superior–subordinate relationship.

Lincoln, as most everyone knows, spent the first three years of the Civil War going through one general after another in a vain attempt to find a capable commander. The emergence of Grant was a godsend. Even before Grant had achieved his first major victory (at Vicksburg), Lincoln said of him, "He doesn't worry and bother me. He isn't shrieking for re-enforcements all the time. He takes what troops we can safely give him . . . and does the best he can with what he has got."

Later, when Grant assumed full command of the Union armies, Lincoln called him "the first General I have had," going on to add, "You know how it has been with all the rest . . . They all wanted me to be the General. . . . I am so glad to find a man who can go ahead without me."

Grant's ability to shoulder responsibility is borne out by his words as well as his deeds. In acknowledging Lincoln's message of good luck before the start of his final campaign, the commanding general wrote to his commander in chief, "Should my success be less than I desire, and expect, the least I can say is, the fault is not with you."

---

risdictional jousts. If someone is encroaching on your territory or refusing you the cooperation you need, make every effort to resolve the matter yourself before dumping it on your boss's desk.

Some problems, of course, belong on your boss's desk. In fact, she may become justifiably annoyed if they do not arrive there. These are issues that involve authority or create implications well beyond your own bailiwick. And there will be problems more closely appertaining to your own position for which you will need or want her help. When you do raise a matter of this kind with your boss, you may want to frame it as a request for advice rather than as a plea for a solution. Instead of saying, "The XYZ company won't pay its last bill" and then waiting for her to say what should be done, you can say, "I can't get the XYZ company to pay its last bill. If you have any suggestions as to how to handle this, I would appreciate them." This approach can elicit a positive reaction from your boss, since you are not asking her to shoulder the responsibility but only seeking to avail yourself of her knowledge and expertise. But even this approach has its limitations; for if you are continually calling on your boss for advice, she will soon tire of giving it, and quite possibly she will tire of you as well. So if the problem is properly yours, then the best course to take is to see that it stays with, and is solved by, you.

DON'T BE TOO EAGER
WITH SUGGESTIONS

Almost every employee has one or more ideas that she fervently believes would greatly improve the operations of her organization. The truly ambitious employee often has several ideas that she wants to offer to her boss. My advice is this: Don't be in too great a hurry to do so.

To begin with, your brilliant idea may not seem quite so stupendous—in fact, it may not even seem very sound—when viewed from your boss's perspective. And remember that her perspective is quite different from yours. It is likely, among other things, to be a good deal broader, encompassing many factors and forces of which you may be only dimly aware. Your idea may upset other plans she has in mind or projects she has in operation. It may create conflicts for her with other members of the organization, including her own boss. At a minimum, implementing your idea is likely to eat into her time, and even if you think it will save her time in the long run, you should remember that managers tend to be short-run-oriented.

There is yet another factor to be considered. A suggestion designed to improve an operation carries with it an implication that the operation needs improvement. In other words, it conveys an overtone of criticism. Accepting the suggestion may require your boss to acknowledge, at least tacitly, an inadequacy in the way she has been running things. Bosses, like the rest of us, have egos; they do not enjoy acknowledging their inadequacies, especially to their subordinates.

None of these caveats means that you should completely refrain from presenting proposals to your boss. Far from it. But you should use discretion when you do present one.

First, choose the time and place for advancing the idea carefully. When a boss is seriously thinking about the problem the proposal is designed to alleviate, this is an obvious occasion for bringing it to her attention. Also, when your boss is in a good mood she is likely to be more receptive. And a suggestion made when you and your boss are alone will often fare better than one advanced when others are present, unless you can be reasonably sure that the others will support your suggestion and that your boss will respond favorably to their endorsement.

Second, package your proposal in such a way that it will cause the least possible disturbance to your boss's regular routine. The usual way to do this is to offer to do most of the work that implementing the proposal will involve. For example, if you think your boss should inform the production department regarding certain customer complaints, offer to draft the letter yourself. If you know your boss well, you can present a draft of such a letter when you make the suggestion. It is usually easier to get a boss to sign something than to compose something.

Finally, don't urge any idea on your boss until you have thought it through *from your boss's perspective.* Effecting organizational change is a good deal like playing billiards. You must take into account not only where the ball will go when you hit it but what other balls it will hit and where *they* will go. The modern organization is an intricate organism with many interlocking and sensitive parts. Being at a higher level, your boss is better able to see and assess these interactions than you are. But by being as alert as possible to all that is going on, by making contacts with others both within and outside of your own area of operation, by studying carefully the memos, house organs, annual reports, trade journals, and other documents that indicate or influence your boss's principles and practices, you can come up with ideas that will benefit both you and your boss—and your organization as well.*

KEEP YOUR BOSS SUPPLIED
WITH USEFUL INFORMATION

While you should avoid bombarding your boss with problems and proposals, you should have far fewer qualms about furnishing him with information. Good bosses especially thrive on information and soon come to respect and rely upon those subordinates who can supply it. Says Robert Garret-

---

*To be sure, there are times when you cannot give a suggestion such careful consideration. Brainstorming sessions and emergencies are two examples that come quickly to mind. However, on such occasions you should generally avoid all-out advocacy of any idea you may happen to come up with. Instead, just lay it on the table, so to speak, indicating that it might be worth considering, while implying that you are not giving it your full endorsement. And indeed you should not be ready to embrace your idea fully on such an occasion, for you will not have had a chance to give it the scrutiny it deserves.

son, former executive vice-president of Carling Breweries, "I have found that the best way for a subordinate to make himself useful and appreciated is by digging up information—figures and facts—concerning proposals being considered, demonstrating interest and sympathy with the ideas favored by the boss, but also presenting new alternatives." And Garretson adds, "Nothing is more appreciated than new information that helps the boss make better decisions."

To be useful, your information should be as objective as possible. This does not mean it must be limited to computer printouts and other kinds of numerical data. Items clipped from newspapers and trade journals can certainly be included. Even anecdotes and gossip picked up in the lunchroom can occasionally prove valuable to your boss. Opinions also meet the standards of objectivity when they are properly presented. When you say that Jones feels the accounting department is not paying bills properly, you are merely reporting a fact, not passing a judgment. However, before reporting Jones's opinion, you can help your boss evaluate its accuracy if you do a rundown on bill payment dates and present it to the boss at the same time that you relay Jones's opinion.

Your information should also be comprehensive, not in the sense of including every single detail but in encompassing or taking into account all the relevant and important aspects of the matter at hand. A failure to do this can create an unbalanced picture of the problem, which in turn can lead to faulty action. When you lack some vital bits of data but feel you should present what you have, indicate what pieces are missing and what steps you are taking to supply them.

As Garretson's statement indicates, information forms the best basis for making a recommendation. In fact, it can often substitute for it. Frequently you will find that the best way of getting a boss to do something is simply to supply him with enough of the proper data. This information may well lead him to come up with the idea on his own. Don't be afraid that this tactic will deprive you of the credit you would have received if you had put forth the idea on your own. If anything, your boss is likely to appreciate you all the more, for you will have reaffirmed his belief in himself as a boss who can make his own decisions.

GIVE YOUR BOSS OPTIONS

For a foreign-born academic, Henry Kissinger's career in American government has been little short of spectacular. He first surfaced to national attention as foreign policy adviser to the late Nelson Rockefeller, then governor of New York, who at that time was seeking the presidency. Rockefeller later recommended Kissinger highly to Richard Nixon, who eventually made him secretary of state. On taking over from Nixon, Gerald Ford made Kissinger's reappointment one of his first items of business. And Ronald Reagan, though compelled to promise his far-right supporters that he would not use Kissinger in such a capacity, nevertheless has found frequent occasions to call upon his services.

One of Kissinger's favorite devices in dealing with presidents and would-be presidents is to offer them options. Instead of proposing a particular policy or course of action, he tries, at least when it comes to major matters, to present them with a list of possibilities and allow them to choose.

Kissinger always makes up such lists carefully. He includes every feasible alternative and scrupulously puts down all its merits and demerits. But he refrains from recommending any particular one.

The advantages of this technique in terms of boss management should be readily apparent. In fact, it incorporates and reflects many of the points made earlier. And it certainly is not limited to the enlarged and exotic arena of foreign affairs. It can be used, and used effectively, in dealing with relatively minor and mundane matters. In short, it can be used by you.

To see how it can work, suppose you are handling employee relations for a small company that has received a large order for its product. As a result of the order, the company has substantially increased its work force. As a further result, its once ample parking lot is now overfilled. Employees have begun competing vigorously and often acrimoniously for the limited number of parking spaces, and just this morning a squabble between two of them for an empty space degenerated into a fist fight.

The problem, you conclude, demands your boss's attention, for any solution that you can think of will require more resources or authority than you possess. But instead of laying the problem in your boss's lap and leaving it for her to resolve, or putting forth a proposed solution and urging her to adopt it, you draw up a list of options. Such options might include enlarging the parking lot, chartering a bus to transport workers to and from the nearest public transit facility, charging a fee for parking and earmarking the proceeds for the employees' recreation fund, organizing car pools, and so on. All of these options have advantages; all of them also have drawbacks. In listing them you carefully but concisely note these advantages and drawbacks. Then, when you call the problem to your boss's attention, you present your list.

This approach does have limitations and liabilities. As should be evident, it may take some time and a good deal of energy as well. Some problems are simply not worth the effort. Other problems may not provide for more than one feasible option. And there is always the tendency for a subordinate to "stack" the list to favor the option he really prefers. A boss who senses this may lose faith in the subordinate's credibility.

Despite such potential drawbacks, the device does have very real attractions. It permits the boss to play a boss's role by making the final decision. Less obviously, it forces the subordinate to consider the problem in a more rounded and thorough manner. The results should benefit both.

MAKE YOUR BOSS LOOK GOOD

You have probably heard the term "Potemkin village." It comes from the cardboard villages that Potemkin was thought to have set up along the Volga to falsely impress Catherine and her distinguished foreign visitors when they came sailing by. Actually, modern historians say that Potemkin never went quite so far, but he did continually stage other displays designed to effect the same purpose, namely, to make his boss look good.

Potemkin was only doing what smart subordinates have always done, though usually in a less spectacular manner. For seeking to make one's boss look good is a well-known and well-accepted tactic in the handbook of boss management. Robert Garretson, for example, cites it as an additional reason for keeping a boss well supplied with useful information. Notes Garretson, "Research that will make the boss look wise is always desirable." He then goes on to suggest ways for enhancing its utilization in this respect. "New information should never be offered in front of a group meeting or conference. Present the facts in advance, preferably in writing, and let the boss do the talking."

In making your boss look good you may on occasion have to let him take credit for something you conceived or created. In most instances you should not find this unduly disconcerting. Although this has been a common cause of complaint for many subordinates, the more able ones have usually gone along with it and sometimes encouraged it. Some have even allowed their bosses to announce the good news while they announce the bad news (a common practice in politics). If your relationship with your superior is reasonably strong and secure, you may find that such policies will actually further your long-term interests and goals. As a wise Englishman once remarked, "A man can do a great deal of good in the world if he is willing to allow others to take the credit for it."

One of the more extraordinary stories of boss management I have come across provides an illustration of this last point. The episode was related some years ago to a private gathering by a UN official who had formerly been the permanent secretary of the Ministry of Education in New Zealand.

Permanent secretaries more or less run their departments in a British-style government, but they cannot make policy. That particular responsibility rests with their immediate superiors, the politically appointed ministers. This permanent secretary, however, had many ideas of his own that he wished to implement. So he compiled his ideas in the form of a book entitled *The Future of Education in New Zealand* and then offered it to his minister to publish under the minister's own name. The minister, eager for the prestige and publicity that authorship of such a book would bring him, accepted the offer with alacrity. The permanent secretary then proceeded to put his ideas into effect with the assurance that he was only carrying out the published policies of his minister. In fact, the minister, having publicly pledged himself to such initiatives, now became their most forceful advocate.

There are, to be sure, bosses whose image one might hesitate to improve, bosses who are so bad that any effort to make them look better becomes tantamount to commiting fraud. We will be taking a look in the next chapter at some of the problems that handling such bosses entails. At this juncture let me conclude by noting that the benefits you can gain by making your boss look good are not limited to the pleasure you may derive from seeing your ideas enacted or to the gratitude you may obtain from the boss herself. There are other, less direct but nonetheless real, advantages to be had.

These other advantages stem from the fact that whether you wish it or not, you will almost certainly be identified with your boss. Consequently, when your boss looks good, you look good; when she is promoted, your chances for promotion improve. And research has shown that a boss who is well paid is more likely to work hard to see that you get a pay raise.

MAKE YOUR BOSS FEEL GOOD

Even the most naive employee usually knows better than to present a troublesome matter to a boss who's in a bad mood unless it is unavoidable. More sophisticated employees realize that this phenomenon has a positive dimension as well, namely, that a boss who is in a good mood is much more approachable and therefore more manageable. Consequently, smart subordinates want their bosses to be happy, not just with their subordinates but with themselves.

As might be expected from what has been observed of him, Cardinal Richelieu was a past master of this practice. He was able, for instance, to interpret his king's often confused emotions to himself and then rationalize them in such a manner as to enable the befuddled monarch to get a grip on himself and feel good about himself. One contemporary remarked how Richelieu daily examined every detail on Louis's face, and if there was a wrinkle out of place, he did not rest until he had put it to rights.

While you may have no wish to go as far as history's great Grey Eminence in this respect, you will usually find it useful to contribute to a state of equanimity in your superior. Even the worst boss will become better, and more reachable, when he is satisfied not only with you but with himself.

Your efforts to make your boss feel good, however, should stop well short of outright flattery. You should not try to please or placate any boss through effusive praise or insincere compliments. Such practices are not just dishonorable but often self-defeating.

Compliments and praise, as modern psychologists like to point out, create at best ambivalent reactions in their recipients. As the late Haim Ginott once noted, "Direct praise of personality, like direct sunlight, is uncomfortable and blinding." It puts the recipient in an artificial and awkward situation, so he usually feels compelled to disavow it or make light of it. It may also make him fearful that he won't be able to live up to the standard that the praise has set for him. If you compliment your boss for something he has done, then the next time, when he may not have done it so well, he may become greatly annoyed, first with himself and then with you.

Flattery also forces the flatterer into an even more awkward situation. It deprives him of the self-respect so useful, if not vital, for the accomplishment of anything worthwhile. It will also cost him the respect of others, including, eventually, the boss himself. A weak boss may like having sycophants as subordinates, but he will rarely if ever accord them much esteem. How can he, since they have apparently placed him so much above them?

Fortunately, there are honorable and effective methods you can employ to make your boss happier with both himself and you. To a great extent they draw upon some of the points we have already explored.

A nineteenth-century British official named Henry Taylor was one of the first to articulate some of these devices. In his still valuable book *The Statesman* Taylor singled out the simple act of listening as one of the safest and most efficacious forms of flattery. "He that can wear the appearance of drinking in every word that is said with thirsty ears," wrote Taylor, "possesses such a faculty for conciliating mankind as a syren might enjoy. For no syren did ever charm the ear of the listener, as the listening ear has charmed the soul of the syren." (Taylor, 1836)

In the preceding chapter we saw how important it was for a superior to listen attentively and actively to a superior. Taylor has now supplied an additional reason for doing so.

But such listening, though valuable in itself, becomes even more effective when followed by an intelligent response. Here, too, Taylor has something valuable to tell us. "Applaud a man's speech at the moment he sits down, and he will take your compliment as exacted by the demands of common civility; but let some space intervene, and then show him that the merits of his speech have dwelt with you when you might have been expected to have forgotten them, and he will remember your compliment for a much longer time than you have remembered his speech." (Taylor, 1836)

You certainly don't have to wait until your boss gives a speech to put this technique into practice. Merely recalling something that she once said on a previous occasion and voicing it at an appropriate moment can prove helpful to your relationship. You don't even have to indicate that you necessarily agree with it. What matters is that you will have shown that you take her statements seriously, which, as a good boss manager, you should in any case do.

Another way to make your boss feel good without bestowing compliments and praise is to relay the favorable responses of others. If your boss gives a speech at a dinner gathering and you and the others at your table all regard it as a good one, don't hesitate to mention *their* reaction to your boss. If you were not at the dinner, you may want to contact one or more of those who were and see if they have anything positive to say. Note that in all these instances you are not voicing an opinion but merely conveying a fact.

Again, you don't have to wait for your boss to make a speech to employ this technique. If your boss chairs a meeting and those who attended came away impressed by one or more things he said or did, you can pass this fact along. Or if he makes a decision and one or more of those who will be affected by it believe it to be a good one, you can convey this bit of information as well. Remember that in transmitting to your boss positive responses to the good things he does, you are encouraging him to do more of the same. You are giving him a nudge in the right direction.

There is yet another form of flattery that you can honorably and often effectively employ in making your boss feel good. This is the flattery of imitation.

S. S. Fader, in her interesting book *Jobmanship,* quotes a former president of the Institute for Motivational Research, Dr. Ernest Dichter, on this point.

"If you know how to reflect an almost duplicate image of some unique aspects of your boss's way of doing things," says Dr. Dichter, "you've got a good start toward presenting yourself in a way that will get your boss to like you and your work. . . . When bosses see some unique aspect of themselves reflected in your behavior, it has to lead to acceptance of you. Otherwise, they would be rejecting themselves, which is contrary to human nature." (Fader, 1978)

Dr. Dichter terms this approach "tactful flattery." And so it is. But you should make sure that any such aspect of your boss that you decide to embrace will in fact work effectively for *you;* otherwise it will backfire. Your boss will tend to think that you've got it all wrong, and rather than entertain doubts about the aspect itself, he will start entertaining doubts about you.

ACCENT THE POSITIVE

Harry Hopkins was once described as a person with "no negation in his character or method of thought." Undoubtedly this quality helped win him the confidence of not just Franklin Roosevelt but the other world leaders he worked with, such as Winston Churchill and Joseph Stalin. For leadership studies show that successful executives, and even some who are not successful, are essentially optimists. They like to believe that problems can be solved and that possibilities can be realized. It should come as no surprise, then, that they look for and expect the same attitude and approach in their subordinates. Roosevelt, for example, disliked recommendations of what not to do; he preferred recommendations of what to do.

This is not to say that superiors seek out subordinates who are pollyannas. As optimistic orientation does not necessarily imply, and certainly does not require, naiveté. Rather, it denotes someone who naturally tends to emphasize the potential rather than the peril in most situations—a person who, as the saying goes, would rather light a candle than curse the darkness. Dwight Eisenhower expressed well what pleases superiors in this respect when he described his own highly valued and longtime aide Major Robert Schultz.

"No crisis, even the small ones that upset most people, ever seems to unhinge him. He is the ingrained optimist who believes things will always work out; and he does everything he can to make them work out." (Eisenhower, 1967)

Much of what we have already examined in regard to subordinate strategy reflects such an approach. In offering your boss options, for instance, you are presenting her with possibilities rather than just problems. However, you can adopt and apply a positive approach to numerous other situations as well.

In speaking about others to your boss, for instance, be quicker to mention their good points than their bad ones. (Unless, perhaps, they are your boss's enemies!) This can be especially valuable when it comes to discussing your colleagues and your own subordinates. When you speak well of your colleagues, you are helping to establish yourself in your bosses's eyes as someone who has adapted well to her team. Bosses like that. When you speak well of your subordinates, you are helping enhance your reputation as someone who can handle people. Bosses tend to like that too.

In those situations where you must call attention to a colleague's or a subordinate's shortcomings, you should still try to retain a positive approach. For example, it's not that your secretary can't type that makes you want to get rid of him but that you have become convinced that he would probably be happier doing something else.

You can often use a positive approach to good effect when it comes to making demands or claims on your boss. Let's say that you have to share a secretary with someone else, but you feel that you need a full-time one for yourself alone. Instead of deluging your boss with complaints about how overworked and backlogged you are, stress how a full-time secretary will enable you to serve her more effectively. Be as specific as you can. If more secretarial assistance will enable you to process 10 percent more orders, reduce the rate of rejects by 10 percent, or reply to customer complaints in three days instead of five, then say so. And if it will permit you to give your boss more assistance with her own work, such as gathering all the data she needs for her monthly production report or even writing the report for her, so much the better. People tend to respond more favorably to requests that favor their own interests, and one of the advantages of the positive approach is that it lends itself to putting requests in just such a form.

The positive approach is not, however, a mere tactic but an attitude, and the more fully you can adopt it, the more able a boss manager you are likely to become. One skillful subordinate I know hardly ever uses such terms as "prob-lem," "crisis," or "setback." He merely describes an event that would normally fall into any of these categories as a "challenge" and then goes on from there to make plans to meet it. Like Eisenhower's Major Schultz, he believes things will work out and does his best to see that they do.

KEEP YOUR PROMISES

Few bosses expect perfection. They realize that everyone does some things better and some things worse than others. So long as the former outweigh the latter, a boss can usually adjust to a subordinate's shortcomings.

What bosses cannot adjust to is uncertainty. If your boss gives you an assignment and you admit you can't do it, then she at least knows where the matter stands and can look for an alternative or discard the project altogether. But if she gives you an assignment and you explicitly avow or tacitly indicate that you can do it and then fail to do so, the chances are that you will have created great difficulties for her and for yourself as well. Not only will your nonperformance up-set her timetable, possibly interfering with other plans and projects that she may have going, but it will make her doubt your reliability. Lack of perfection is one thing; lack of pre-dictability is quite another.

"When a boss asks a subordinate to do something that is beyond the experience and skill of the subordinate," says Robert Garretson, "it is always best, I think, for the sub-ordinate to state frankly what he doesn't know and what he would have to learn." Garretson goes on to suggest that the subordinate might indicate a desire to acquire the skills or knowledge necessary for the execution of the assignment and that, in many instances, the boss could help him do so. But in any case, the subordinate should not be afraid to admit his inadequacy.

When you do make a commitment that you honestly feel at the time you can fulfill and then find you cannot do so, you should alert your boss as soon as possible. Many a subordinate has held off doing so, fearing his boss's displeasure while hoping that something will miraculously happen to change the situation. This is generally poor practice. Any annoyance your boss is likely to display over discovering that you cannot keep your promise is likely to be far less if she learns about it sooner rather than later. The earlier you take your lumps, the lighter they are likely to be.

"It is better to be known for making honest mistakes," writes William Delaney, "than to be known as someone whose word cannot be relied on." And he adds, "We all make mistakes; it's how we handle them that matters."

DON'T STAY LATE; COME IN EARLY

While work that produces desirable results may count the most, hard work in itself pleases bosses. Any extra effort on your part shows enthusiasm and dedication, inspires others to work harder, and flatters the boss, since you are, after all, working hard for him.

In your desire to demonstrate your commitment to your job and to do all or more than what is expected of you, you will probably on occasion have to put in some additional hours. When this occurs, insert these hours at the beginning rather than at the end of the day. Instead of staying late to finish a project, go home, retire a bit earlier than usual, and come in earlier the following day. For more than one reason, this is usually the best way to put in extra time.

The most apparent advantage of such a strategy is that it enables you to perform the extra work when you are fresh instead of tired. But another advantage is that it looks better. As Robert Schoenberg points out, coming in early says to the boss, "I'm eager to get started," while staying late says, "I didn't get everything done."

Some successful subordinates make it an everyday practice to show up on the job ahead of time. One of them is James Medeiros, who made what would normally be a dif-

ficult transition, moving from a position as associate professor of political science in an undistinguished university to
that of assistant vice-president of one of the nation's largest
insurance companies. Says Medeiros of his early-to-arrive
habit, "While others are just getting the sand out of their
eyes, I have my work all lined up and am ready to go."

DON'T GET TOO CLOSE TO YOUR BOSS

Ideally, you will manage to build a strong and supportive
relationship with your boss, one that may carry over into occasional contacts outside the work place and one that will
continue after you have moved on to fresher fields. The relationship should not, however, reach the point where you
become closely concerned and involved with each other's personal lives.

I say this realizing that fast friendships do occasionally
develop between superior and subordinate that produce considerable benefits to both. The problem is that such closeness
produces perils as well. You will generally find it safer to
maintain some degree of distance. A cordial relationship
should be prized, but a relationship that involves sharing intimate secrets and discussing personal problems should normally be discouraged.

There are many reasons why this is so, some of them
quite obvious. All have their basis in the fact that you
and your boss are not really equals, at least not within the
organizational context in which your relationship takes
place. Intimate friendship, however, has an equalizing effect and therefore tends to distort and disturb the superior-
subordinate liaison. Suppose your boss tells you a secret that,
if revealed, could cause him great injury. You might at first
feel flattered and even triumphant at such a display of trust.
Indeed, your boss has actually given you a weapon that you
could use against him should you so desire. But the chances
are that your boss will sooner or later regret having exposed
and, in a sense, lowered himself and may come to see you as

a potential threat. Such sentiments hardly make for a satisfactory relationship.

Even when a boss's confidences are limited to organizational matters they can still be troublesome. For the more deeply you immerse yourself in his concerns, the more you implicitly if not explicitly commit yourself to them. And while you normally will want to stand and fight on his side, you will also want to retain some freedom to think for yourself and to act on your own.

Pursuing this point a bit further, you may find it in your best interest to limit your interactions with your boss. To be sure, many a subordinate has ingratiated himself with, and wielded considerable influence over, a boss by constantly being at the boss's elbow. Hitler's Martin Borman comes to mind. Moreover, many another subordinate has ended up overlooked and overridden because he was not around the boss enough to preserve and protect his interests. Nevertheless, constant contact remains a two-edged sword that can as easily, if not more easily, cut against you as for you.

The more you are around your boss, the more demands he is likely to make on you. This may lead to unfulfilled promises on your part, which in turn can lead to unfulfilled expectations on his. Also, when two people spend much time together they inevitably end up knowing each other's foibles and flaws. This can jeopardize your position not just in exposing your weaknesses to your boss but in exposing his weaknesses to you. It has been said that no man can be a hero to his valet, and bosses, to some degree, want to be heroes or heroines to those who serve them. Otherwise they cannot elicit the respect so vital to playing a leadership role.

Constant contact also consumes time that you might better spend doing other things. Any boss worth working for will want to see more from you than your face. While you are busy interacting with her, someone else may be out fulfilling her plans and solving her problems.

Finally, hovering around your boss too much can and probably will earn you a reputation as the boss's pet. And while such a reputation may prompt co-workers to accede more readily to your wishes, it may also cause them to dislike and distrust you. Some may even look for ways to undermine your position. Anyone who bases his standing in an organization solely on his standing with his boss has generally rooted himself in very thin soil that can easily wash away.

The proper and least perilous course to pursue, then, lies along the middle way. Avoid becoming either obscure or obvious. Keep your boss aware of your existence without continually confronting him with it. As England's Charles II once said of a valued aide, "Sidney Godolphin is never in the way and never out of the way." This may be one reason why long after Charles and even some of his successors had departed from the scene, Sidney Godolphin was still helping direct the affairs of the British government.*

DON'T MAKE YOUR BOSS YOUR MENTOR

Mentoring has aroused a lot of attention in recent years, inspiring a slew of books, articles, and seminars. Its sudden popularity probably stems from the growing awareness of and respect for Japanese managerial practices, of which mentoring is a fixed feature, as well as from the long overdue influx of women into organizational life (see box).

Choosing and cultivating a mentor makes a good deal of sense for anyone seeking a successful organizational career. But even a brief review of its various functions and facets should show that mentoring differs decidedly from supervising and is therefore best performed by someone other than a superior.

---

*It is interesting to note that Richelieu managed to exercise careful control over Louis XIII without spending much time in the king's presence. As novelist-historian Louis Auchincloss points out, a constant companionship would have left the cardinal with insufficient time to do his own work. It might also have continually reminded the monarch of his own greatly inferior gifts. Comments Auchincloss, "The kind of devotion they had for each other—and it existed—probably flourished best in memory and reflection."

One final historical note: Grant had earned the full trust and confidence of Lincoln before he ever met him.

Mentoring is an almost wholly supportive relationship. Unlike your supervisor, your mentor should be primarily concerned not with what you can do for him but with what he can do for you. His main aim, as far as you are concerned, should be to further your career.

In playing this role, a mentor can not only help you with some of the problems you might not want to bring to your boss but also assist you with some of the problems you might have with your boss. And with a mentor you can usually share more personal matters as well. Indeed, emotion, feelings, and

MENTORING THE MANAGERIAL WOMAN

Mentoring helps women more than men, for women usually enter work organizations less well grounded in and less well prepared for their precepts and practices. This is the conclusion reached by Nancy W. Collins after surveying over 400 upwardly mobile working women. In her book *Professional Women and Their Mentors* (Prentice-Hall, 1983), Collins points out that such activities as team sports give men experience in taking orders and working with others that women often lack. Good mentoring, she says, can help make up for such deficiencies.

Nearly 95 percent of the women she surveyed had found their mentors helpful to their careers, and over half of them described the relationship as "very valuable." However, virtually all those who had chosen their bosses as mentors regretted having done so.

Most of these women's mentors were male, but, says Collins, that should soon change. More women are moving into upper-level positions and, more importantly perhaps, are starting to feel secure enough in such positions to help other women advance as well.

The growing availability of women mentors should do much to alleviate one problem that affected some 20 percent of the women in her sample. These were the ones who reported having had sex with their mentors. All of them advised against it.

sentiment—all have a distinct place in a mentoring relation-ship. As psychologist Daniel J. Levinson observes, a good mentor is an admixture of a good parent and a good friend.

The relationship need not be totally one-sided. How-ever, given your different positions and roles, the things you do for your mentor may not always fall into the category of organizational affairs. In one instance, a young woman helped her middle-aged male mentor go through the trauma of a difficult divorce and then provided him with a few point-ers on how to date again.

If your relationship with your mentor becomes stagnant or sour, you can always end it and look for another mentor instead. In fact, you may find it advisable to seek out new mentors as you move upward while still maintaining cordial contact with your previous ones. The study of successful business executives mentioned earlier (see Chapter 1) showed that all those who made it to the top had developed several such mentoring relationships along the way.

Such considerations as these should make evident why your mentor should not be your superior or even be within your chain of command. The relationship almost always works best when neither party to the arrangement has a direct organizational impact on the other. This leaves them free to view each other as individuals and, proceeding from there, to become helpmates and friends.

DON'T BE DISLOYAL, UNLESS . . .

A visitor once asked Franklin Roosevelt why he had seemed to brighten up when Harry Hopkins entered the office. Roo-sevelt replied by pointing out that almost everyone who came through his door wanted something from him. But Hopkins came in with the sole purpose of serving him. Such loyalty was something Roosevelt not only valued but needed.

Other bosses have felt the same way. Eisenhower ex-pressed it well when he noted that "whatever our position, whatever power we exercise under the weight of responsibility, we need familiar faces around us as much as we need expert opinion or wise counsel. Although the faces at times may be reminders of past tests endured and passed rather than a guarantee of success, they are heartening. They show loyalty, visible evidence that one does not stand alone."

Eisenhower himself was a loyal subordinate even to a boss he did not personally like, Douglas MacArthur. Loyalty to superiors also characterized the careers of the other successful boss managers described in this book, such as John Raskob, Alfred Sloan, and Andrew Carnegie. The Duke of Wellington, when pressured to sign a treaty that he did not favor and that he knew would cause him trouble, did so without complaint or protest, later explaining, "I have eaten of the King's salt; and, therefore, I conceive it to be my duty to serve with unhesitating zeal and cheerfulness when and wherever the King or his government may think proper to employ me." When, prior to the battle of Waterloo, London sent him some politically-connected and incompetent staff officers, the Iron Duke shrugged his shoulders and replied, "I will do the best I can with the instruments which you have sent to assist me."*

In recent years a plethora of novels, plays, and movies have appeared that tend to discredit the role of loyalty in the business world. They depict the executive suite as a sort of vipers' nest with rewards going to the most ruthless and underhanded. Such fictionalized accounts are based more on fantasy than on fact, for disloyalty is customarily frowned upon in business, as it is in sports, politics, and other areas of human activity. The Center for Creative Leadership in its study of derailed executives—promising executives who never fulfilled their promise—found betrayal of trust to have been the downfall of many. Backbiting and back-stabbing one's boss have more frequently obstructed than opened up avenues to advancement.

Disloyalty is first of all dishonorable. To work for a

*Moving from history to literature, we find an interesting observation stating the converse of this point in Charles Dickens's *Our Mutual Friend*. It is "the incompetent servant, by whomever employed," notes Dickens, who "is almost always against his employer."

boss while working against her is to live a lie. In speaking and behaving one way before your boss and another way behind her back, you establish yourself in the eyes of everyone as a practitioner of deceit. You cannot help losing some respect, including a good deal of self-respect, in the process.

When you manifest disloyalty to your boss you also make others wonder how much they can trust you. Even if they agree thoroughly with your negative feelings about your superior, when they hear you articulate them, they cannot help acquiring some negative feelings about you. For if you are willing to be disloyal to your boss, how can they ever be sure that you won't someday be disloyal to them?

A similar example is that of lawyers who work for a time for the government and then leave to take better-paying positions with business firms whose activities they had previously helped to regulate. You might think their desire to win lucrative positions with these firms at a later date would have caused these lawyers to go easy on such firms when they were working for the government. That rarely happens, however, for most companies would think twice before hiring such an attorney. After all, a lawyer who "threw" a case when he was on the government's side might just as easily do the same when he was on the company's side. Often the more effectively the lawyer represents the government, the more respect he reaps from the company that bears the brunt of his efforts.*

Disloyalty to your boss can create problems for you not only with fellow workers and future bosses but also with your own subordinates. Research studies have repeatedly shown that those who work in an organization tend to take their cues on how to behave from their superiors. If your subor-

---

*This does not mean the crossover of lawyers from government to private industry does not pose problems. It certainly does, and in the past few years some steps have been taken to remedy them. For example, lawyers must now wait for a certain number of years before representing clients before agencies that previously employed them. The frequent crossover of assistant district attorneys to the ranks of criminal lawyers also poses problems that have as yet received little recognition and have prompted almost no action.

dinates perceive you as disloyal to your superior, they will find it much easier to be disloyal to you.

Disloyalty also exposes you to more direct dangers. You may inadvertently let loose a verbal or facial expression that indicates your true feelings. Or your boss may hear of your bad faith from others. Many bosses have their own informal channels of communication at all levels of their organization. In any case, working for a boss whom you really want to work against places you in a stressful situation that is hardly conducive to your organizational effectiveness, let alone your health and happiness.

Finally, the disloyal employee must forgo the many advantages that only true loyalty can provide. The most important of these advantages is increased influence over the superior, for the latter will be more inclined to heed the advice of a subordinate whose loyalty has been shown to be fast and firm. To borrow another example from history, John Rawlins could, and often did, argue vigorously with his chief, Ulysses S. Grant, without ever endangering his position as Grant's number-one aide. He could often persuade Grant to modify and sometimes even reverse a decision. For Grant knew that however critical or condemnatory Rawlins might be of him in any particular situation, his aide had no other purpose than to further his superior's well-being.

Having taken all these factors into account, it must yet be said that all too many bosses are difficult if not impossible to admire or like. They may be brutal despots or fussy nit-pickers. They may be insincere or indecisive or simply incompetent. And occasionally they can be or seem to be all these things. So what do you do?

Specific problems along these lines plus those occasions when disloyalty is acceptable and even necessary will be dealt with in the next chapter. At this juncture, let me simply suggest that you try to find features in your boss you can respect and that you try to build on them. Virtually every boss, like virtually every other human being, has some positive aspects. Make an inventory of those your boss has, and then keep them in mind as you seek to establish a good or at least a workable superior–subordinate relationship.

If you look hard enough, you may find that even your boss's negative qualities have a favorable dimension. If he is brutal and blunt, then this also means that he is direct and to the point. If he vacillates, then at least he is not headstrong and reckless. If he is a fusspot, then he probably does not tolerate shoddy work.

While endeavoring to think positively about your boss—and admittedly, with some bosses it is an endeavor that requires a good deal of effort—you can also take a more positive view of your situation. For a bad boss presents a challenge that can and in fact should prod you into developing your own technical and organizational skills. As to the latter, an insincere boss will require you to learn how to interpret slight nuances in speech or behavior. A tyrannical or indecisive boss will force you to develop your skills of persuasion. And a boss who fails to protect your interests will compel you to protect them yourself. A bad boss can actually do a lot for his subordinates.

You should always hesitate to run down or ridicule your boss to others in the organization. If he is a hard-driving despot, you can say he sets a tough pace. If he is a nitpicker, you can refer to him as exacting or meticulous in his standards. If he is indecisive, you can speak of him as cautious. If he is really as bad as you believe, others will soon see what

A CASE OF OVERLOYALTY

A flu-ridden executive once decided, over the protestations of his wife, to rise from his sickbed and go to the office to attend an important meeting. An hour or so later his wife called his office to check on his condition. His secretary said he was at the meeting and then answered his wife's questions as to how her husband looked and acted, reassuring her that he did not seem to be in bad shape. As the wife got ready to hang up, the secretary said to her, "It was so nice of you to call."

As might be expected, the executive spent several hours that evening pacifying a highly irritated spouse.

you mean, especially if you provide examples. There is seldom any need to be more explicit.

But if loyalty, even when it lacks any feelings of admiration or affection, forms the foundation for good superior–subordinate relations, it too can be carried too far. If you become too zealous in serving your superior, you may neglect and damage not only your own interests but your superior's interests as well.

The overly loyal employee often becomes too protective. He may shield his superior from people she should meet and problems she should confront. Such an employee can also become too uncritical, responding with approval and applause to every decision or action the superior makes or takes, no matter how unwise. Loyalty, like everything else in life, has its limits, and a smart subordinate will take care not to transcend them (see "A Case of Overloyalty").

COPING
WITH PROBLEMS
5

Many years ago Frank Capra made a movie about a middle-aged office clerk who suddenly and unexpectedly learns that he has inherited a million dollars. On receiving the news, the clerk, played superbly by Charles Laughton, methodically puts away his papers and pencils, rises from his desk, and, oblivious of the stares of his fellow workers, strides out of the office. In the same resolute manner he proceeds down the corridor, mounts the stairs, and enters another office. There he quickly passes two secretaries, and ignoring their cries of "You can't go in there!" he opens a door revealing a long spacious office with a stern-faced older man sitting at a desk at the far end. With dignity and determination, the clerk marches down to the desk, stops just in front of it, sticks out his tongue, and emits a loud raspberry. At long last, he has achieved his dream of telling off his boss.

Like most genuinely comic incidents, this one is rooted in reality. For the superior–subordinate relationship is not *naturally* conducive to harmony and bliss. Psychologists tell us that the best relationships are based on equality, and although the inequality between superior and subordinate may have narrowed in most organizations in recent years, a gap continues to separate them. Movies may no longer depict clerks achieving nirvana by sticking out their tongues at

---

TOLERATING THE INTOLERABLE

Is there a dreadful boss in your future? Probably, if a survey of seventy-three successful business executives offers any indication. The survey, as published in the January 1984 issue of *Psychology Today,* found that fifty-four, or well over two-thirds, of these business leaders had served under at least one intolerable boss while working their way to the top.

What made these bosses so bad? The answers varied. Some were procrastinators and decision dodgers; others were tyrants; still others were nitpickers. Many simply lacked basic integrity.

Most of the executives surveyed developed techniques and tactics to cope with their intolerable bosses. As one of them put it, "If he is a roller-coaster [that is, subject to sharp ups and downs in mood], catch him on the upswing. If you must differ on one matter, be supportive on several others; if your clash with him is personal, keep everything on a business basis; try to confront the boss only on important points."

Most of the executives felt their intolerable bosses taught them two very valuable lessons. The first was how to exercise patience and cope with adversity. The second was how to manage their own subordinates better by seeing their superior manage them and their co-workers so badly.

Only four of the fifty-four quit outright. As one of the majority who had stayed the course observed, "No boss is really intolerable because you can learn something from every one of them."

bosses, but in the comic strip world Dagwood Bumstead is still having his troubles with Mr. Dithers.

The suggestions presented thus far will, it is hoped, help reduce the tensions in your own relationships with superiors, but they will certainly not eliminate them entirely. For even the best of boss-managers experience such difficulties from time to time. In the words of the old-time salesman, they go with the territory.

Problems with bosses vary from individual to individual and from situation to situation. However, some kinds of problems occur more frequently than others, and while few of them lend themselves to easy, ready-made resolutions, there are some general approaches that have proven helpful.

HOW DO I TELL BAD NEWS TO MY BOSS?

New York City's colorful mayor Fiorello La Guardia customarily fired anyone who brought him bad news. And New York City's controversial commissioner Robert Moses fired on the spot his close aide of thirty years, George Spargo, when Spargo told Moses that his 1960 World's Fair was going to end up in the red. While La Guardia usually called his dismissed aides the following day to ask why they had not come to work, and while Moses eventually hired Spargo back, reacting to bad news by venting displeasure on those who disclose it is a fairly widespread phenomenon that is by no means limited to city officials in New York. So the task of conveying such news is one that a subordinate should undertake with caution.

One way of handling such a situation is to find someone else to do it for you. Even Richelieu, despite his strong hold over Louis XIII, regularly resorted to this expedient. However, like the solutions to so many vexing problems, this one is easier said than done. People who will want to spare you the boss's wrath by taking it upon themselves are likely to be in short supply. And if you do maneuver or manipulate someone into doing so, they may, and indeed should, bear you a grudge that could come back to haunt you at a later date. At times you may be able to seize on someone, such as a client or other outside party, who has nothing to lose in performing the task, and when such people are available you may want to make use of them. But don't count on this stratagem as a steady solution.

A much more reliable strategy is prevention. This involves anticipating the kinds of bad news that may arise and then developing ways for your boss to learn about it without having to learn it from you. The most common means for doing this is a management information system. Such a system should automatically reveal much of the bad news that your boss will need to know. To the extent that you can, make sure that your boss is equipped with such a system and that the system itself is equipped to provide the necessary data. Short of such a full-scale information system, or supplementary to it, various standardized procedures can be put into effect for the same purpose.

Unfortunately, no management information system or standardized procedure is likely to disclose in a timely manner that Bill Jones has just walked off the job while in the midst of a crucial assignment, or that the XYZ company has just canceled its multi-million-dollar order. There will always be unwelcome developments that must be brought to the boss's attention personally.

There are three fairly well-known ways of mitigating the effect of bad news. The first, and the most obvious, is to play down its import. For example, an employee of a large accounting firm says that when he fails to get an order, he often tells his boss that they are probably just as well off, for the client would have been more bother than he was worth.

The difficulty with such a stratagem is, however, almost as obvious. Seeking to shrug off an unwelcome development will scarcely raise you in your superior's esteem if she views it quite differently. It could, on the contrary, make you look naive as well as self-serving. Downplaying bad news works best when legitimate reasons exist for doing so. If you can come up with such reasons, fine, but otherwise tread carefully in seeking to depreciate its impact.

The second commonly used tactic is to find some good news to report along with the bad. Sometimes such good news can be extracted directly from the bad. For example, the accounting firm employee previously mentioned says that on other occasions when a job doesn't work out he may tell his boss how much he and his colleagues learned by working on it. Actually, every negative development can prove instructive or helpful in some way, and you may want to bring out these positive aspects when you reveal the development to your boss. But two caveats are in order: (1) Be specific. Pinpoint these positive effects rather than mentioning them in general terms. (2) Do not exaggerate their value. If your firm has invested heavily in a new product that has failed miserably, your boss is not likely to appreciate hearing that the lessons learned were worth the costs involved.

When the good news is not part of the bad, it presents a further problem. Should you announce it before or after the unpleasant information? Organizational researcher and theorist Chris Argyris found in a company he studied that its executives in presenting reports to the president always gave the good news before the bad. However, you may want to think carefully before adopting such a rule, for the reverse procedure may serve you better. When the good news is presented after the bad it can provide relief and help you to end the encounter on a more positive note. But again, don't exaggerate its importance. If it does not really outweigh the bad, don't pretend that it does.

The third tactic utilizes one of the practices recommended earlier for everyday use: provide your boss with options. If you have just learned that a rival company has landed the contract your company had been hoping to get, pause for a moment before telling your boss and try to frame possible courses of action that you or your boss can take to mitigate the loss. Bosses confronted with a crisis almost always feel a desperate desire to do something. If you can offer some useful ideas of action that could be taken, you may provide your boss with a psychological outlet as well as an organizational service.

But while it may be permissible and often desirable to delay the delivery of even urgent bad news for a brief moment while you weigh its impact and assess alternatives, you should rarely, if ever, hold it back because you fear your boss's reaction. Although misfortunes and mistakes sometimes correct themselves, most often they do not. Left unattended, they usually get worse. Conveying ill tidings can be distasteful and occasionally even dangerous, but suppressing them can be disastrous for all concerned, not least of all for you.

Finally, one kind of bad news you should make sure to be the first to reveal to your boss. This is the news that reflects badly on yourself. By being the first to disclose it you can to some degree shape and control it. You may even impress your boss favorably with your willingness to acknowledge and inform her of it. At a minimum, you will be able to observe her reaction at first hand, and this can help you proceed more intelligently to overcome its ill effects.

HOW CAN I SELL MY GREAT IDEA TO MY BOSS?

The first thing you should do is make sure it really *is* great. Try it out on your mentor and colleagues, and possibly your friends and spouse as well. The idea that seems so dazzling to you may look quite different to them. It may be—and this often happens—that your idea is a great or at least a good idea in all respects but one, and that one flaw may spell its doom. At all events, let others pick it apart before you let your boss do so.

Another useful procedure is to put your idea in writing, carefully listing all its features, possible methods of implementation, and the problems it may involve, as well as the payoffs you expect it to yield. Do this irrespective of whether you wish to present it to your boss or others in written form. Simply writing it down now will force you to think it through in a more comprehensive and systematic manner. You will probably see, or see more clearly, aspects of it that had remained vague or unnoticed when it was still simply a notion floating around in your mind. Francis Bacon once said that an index chiefly profits the person who compiled it. The same can be said for a written idea.

If, after you have put your idea in writing and discussed it with fellow workers or friends, it still seems sound to you, then you can start to think about presenting it to your boss. But don't be in a hurry to do so. Scout out the terrain first. You can, for instance, merely mention at an appropriate moment the problem or one of the problems it is designed to address and note his reaction. Is this a problem that concerns him? Is he likely to be on the lookout for some new way of handling it? You might then float a trial balloon, indicating that you have been doing some thinking on the subject and describing just what your lines of thought on it have been.

When it comes time to unveil the proposal, present it in terms that will appeal to your boss's preoccupations and proclivities. Never lose sight of the fact that it is what your boss thinks is important, not what you think is important, that counts. Always keep her interests and involvements in mind, in the order of priority she has assigned to them.

In his book *The Art of Getting Your Own Sweet Way* Philip B. Crosby offers a fictitious but realistic example of the importance of this point. He describes an analyst from headquarters trying to persuade one of a company's most popular and powerful branch managers to accept a new system. The analyst gets nowhere until he stops trying to sell the system and instead starts to listen—to the man himself and to others as well. He learns that the balky branch manager wishes he had more time to spend on community service activities. Taking this clue as his cue, so to speak, the analyst gets the manager to accept the new system by stressing its value as a time-saving measure.

One of history's more intriguing instances of a subordinate successfully using such an approach occurred in Nazi Germany in 1944. Hitler had just issued a directive for the retreating German armies to blow up every French city and town they were abandoning before the Allied advance. Albert Speer, one of Hitler's closest and more civilized associates, was appalled at the command. Knowing that his boss still believed the war could be won, Speer persuaded him to rescind the order by pointing out that they would need these cities and towns intact when the tide turned and they reoccupied the country.

Before you try to sell your idea to your boss, you should have anticipated most of her objections through careful advance preparation. You should particularly have taken into account two factors. The first is what parties and interests both within and outside of your boss's area of authority will be affected by the idea and what their responses will be. The second is the costs, not only in money but in lost prestige, wasted time and energy, and so on, that will be incurred if the idea misfires. Too often a subordinate with a suggestion to sell neglects both these factors. Yet they are likely to be paramount in the superior's mind. If you can show that your proposal will generate a largely positive response from those affected, or, if the response will be negative, that it can easily be overcome, and if you can also show that the costs of its failure will be minimal, then you will have advanced a long way toward gaining her approval.

If your boss still hesitates, you may want to suggest consulting others she respects who you believe will support your idea. In the meantime, you should have marshaled as much convincing documentation as possible in its behalf, including any examples of how your idea, or something like it, is working or has worked elsewhere.

But always be careful of overselling. Do not press your case too hard. This is why it is usually best to lead up to your proposal gradually over a period of time. If your boss still seems reluctant, you may wish to lower your demands, requesting a trial experiment or even just some further study. Try to avoid presenting the proposal in a form that requires a decisive and immediate yes or no. Also try to present it in such a way that its rejection will not be construed as a rejection of you. Unless your idea is a matter of overriding concern to you, don't stake your future effectiveness, and possibly your future employment, on its acceptance.

Finally, if your boss does buy your suggestion, be prepared for less than enthusiastic praise even if it works as well as you have promised. In fact, if you sell too many ideas to your boss, and if they work too successfully, you may find him apt to take you down a peg or two. This results from a crucial aspect of boss behavior that subordinates often overlook.

Bosses in some respects have more ego problems than those who work under them. Bosses are not supposed to make mistakes. What's more, they are supposed to tell their subordinates what to do, not let their subordinates tell them. This last aspect is especially germane here. When your boss adopts one of your suggestions, he is reversing the stereotype of the superior–subordinate relationship since he is in effect taking direction from you. He may, therefore—especially if his ego is a bit brittle, as all too many bosses' egos are—feel he has lost some face and seek to redress the situation by putting you in your place.

This should not unduly alarm you. A little bit of humiliation by your boss, possibly in the form of a slighting remark or two when others are present, can be viewed as a natural reflex resulting from his having listened to you. Louis frequently did this to Richelieu, as did Nixon to Kissinger. Within this context, such behavior can be looked upon as a sign of success in the fine art of boss management.*

---

*Some really shrewd boss managers have avoided even these minor backlashes by persuading their superiors not just to accept their idea but to believe that the idea came from the superior himself. This is one of the secrets behind the amazing career of William Pitt, who at the age of twenty-four became prime minister of Great Britain and who, with one brief interruption, remained prime minister until his death at the age of forty-seven. In launching both at home and abroad a large number of new programs and policies, Pitt managed to make George III believe that he was only carrying out his monarch's wishes.

HOW DO I KEEP MY BOSS FROM GOING AHEAD WITH A BAD IDEA?

Although this problem bears an obvious relationship to the preceding one, it nevertheless requires a somewhat different approach. While a boss may merely resist an employee's effort to persuade him to do something the employee wants done, he may resent an employee's attempt to prevent him from doing something that *he* wants done. The latter initiative, then, requires some truly delicate handling if it is to achieve its purpose instead of jeopardizing your relationship with your superior.

Before embarking on such a mission, you should make sure the idea or decision is really a bad one. From your boss's perspective, the idea may yield many more benefits and far fewer ill consequences than it might seem from where you sit. Make sure you understand not just what your boss wants to do but why she wants to do it, what she sees as its advantages, and what she regards as its drawbacks.

Your first task, then, is to consider the matter carefully, bringing into play all that you have learned about your boss. Your second task is to ask questions.

Your questions can do more than elicit information; they can also indirectly raise the objections you have to the proposal or project. Phrased carefully, they should enable you to get your points across without arousing your boss's ire or causing her to become defensive.

One of the more successful subordinates I have known is a master of this approach. Deeply involved in politics for many years, he managed to get along so well with all the diverse leaders of his state's majority party that they eventually made him the youngest party chairman in the state's history. This particular fellow almost never argues with anyone, be it superior or subordinate. Instead he smiles pleasantly and proceeds to ask questions. By the time he has finished, he will have put all his objections to the proposed course of action on the table and forced the proposer to consider them. Yet the atmosphere has at all times remained warm and friendly.

If, after all your questions have been posed, your boss has not budged from her position, you should focus your attention on the merits of what she wants to do. Virtually any idea, no matter how faulty or how flawed, will have attractive aspects. You should make sure that you see them and that your boss sees that you see them. It is, after all, her idea, and as such it deserves respect. Even if the idea comes from another source, your boss, in adopting it, has invested it with her own ego and prestige. You should never treat such an investment lightly.

Now comes the hard part: making your boss see that whatever merits the idea has, its drawbacks far outweigh them. You can usually do this more effectively, both in terms of influencing your boss and in terms of protecting your own position, by calling on others for help.

If you believe the proposal will create too much adverse publicity, offer to check it with public relations. If you think it will cost too much, offer to go over the figures with a cost accountant or someone else in a position to provide the pertinent data. If you fear that it will raise a rumpus at city hall, offer to sound out a friendly city councilor. Whatever you find out you should report faithfully to your boss without doctoring it up to reflect your own skeptical view. If the idea is as bad as you think, somewhere along the line one or more other sources will probably bring your objections to light.

While you are doing this you should be thinking of possible alternatives to the course of action that you are trying to block. If at all possible, such alternatives should incorporate some of the more attractive aspects of the original. Presenting them at an appropriate moment will give your boss a chance to salvage something from the situation and to retain her role as decision maker and doer.

Should you succeed in bringing your boss around to your point of view, you should scrupulously refrain from showing elation. Since your boss obviously thought highly of the proposal, policy, or project, having to abandon it will not be a happy occasion for her. It should not be a happy one for you either.

But suppose you fail, as you undoubtedly will on some occasions, to change her mind. What do you do then?

Unless what your boss is doing is illegal, immoral, or decidedly dangerous to you, your employees, or the organization itself—and we will be taking a longer look at these issues shortly—you should go along with it. You should work for its success, not sluggishly or sullenly, but with as much enthusiasm as you can muster.

In 1983 I asked a regional director for the Department of Housing and Urban Development (HUD) what he thought of Reagan's policies. Since the conservative president had imposed some tough restraints on HUD's activities, and since the official I was interviewing was one of the agency's career civil servants and a liberal Democrat to boot, I anticipated a volley of vehement criticism. Yet I found that while he certainly did not like the president's policies, he was quite willing to go along with them. In fact, he could even see some merits in them. He pointed out, as an example, that the department's administrative staff had probably become a bit bloated over the years and that Reagan's austerity measures were helping to correct this. There was no question that he preferred different and more generous policies, but there was also no question that he could live with and cheerfully carry out those that the White House had promulgated.

Throughout history, other successful subordinates have taken the same tack. When Harry Hopkins failed to persuade Roosevelt to keep a certain relief program going, he set about dismantling it as quickly and efficiently as he could. When George Schultz felt that one of President Nixon's policies was unwise, he avoided making too great an issue of it. If the president really wanted it done, then Schultz did it as well as he could. As a result, the former business school dean was promoted from secretary of labor to head of the Office of Management and Budget. And since Nixon never asked him to do anything that was morally or legally controversial, Schultz escaped the Watergate scandal unscathed and thus could return to Washington to serve another Republican president as secretary of state, the third-highest-ranking position in the national government.

But, you may now ask, how can I ethically defend a decision or promote a policy of which I do not approve? In so doing won't I make myself a liar?

Not necessarily. It depends on how you do it. In countries with a parliamentary system, for example, government policies are decided by the cabinet. It frequently happens that one or more members of the cabinet will disagree with a particular decision. Yet they must support it or resign. Occasionally, one or more cabinet members will resign over an issue, but most often the dissenters go along with the majority. However, in speaking of it, a dissenting cabinet member will use such phrases as "my government believes" or "our policy is." She will thus avoid giving the decision her personal stamp of approval. And since the majority of the cabinet members who voted for it will speak of it in the same way, the dissent usually goes unnoticed.

You can follow a similar course in defending any decision you may happen to disagree with. "My boss believes" or "my department feels" are the kinds of phrases you can legitimately use to maintain your self-respect. No sensible person should think less of you for exerting every effort to make a bad decision yield the best results. On the contrary, they may value you all the more, especially if "they" happen to be your boss. For a willingness to work hard at implementing something you did not want to see initiated in the first place provides an acid test of loyalty. As Robert Garretson puts it:

> The subordinate should be completely loyal, even when he may disagree with what his boss is planning to do. . . . After all, no boss is always right. He can make mistakes. Neither is any subordinate always right. Loyalty means working together, taking into account different views that are bound to exist.

WHEN SHOULD I STOP BEING LOYAL TO MY BOSS?

As noted earlier, your loyalty may end when your boss does something illegal, immoral, or dangerous to you, your employees, or the organization itself. Let us examine each of these situations in turn.

When a boss engages in clearly illegal or immoral activity, you should take steps to counteract it or, at a minimum, remove yourself from his area of authority. You should do this even if you are not directly involved in such actions and cannot be formally held responsible for them. For, ethical considerations aside, your boss's behavior will almost certainly tarnish you as well. You may throw up your hands and exclaim, "I am not my boss's keeper," but others will not be willing to let you off so lightly. They will assume either that you knew about it and just didn't care or that you didn't know about it and therefore are pretty dumb. You should not expose yourself to either charge.

You should also think of taking action when your boss has embarked on a policy, project, or program that is virtually certain to have grave consequences to your organization. Here, too, your self-interest is directly at stake. While you risk gaining a reputation for disloyalty in moving to counteract him, you may risk your reputation for intelligence, decisiveness, and overall loyalty to the organization itself in allowing him to proceed unchecked. You may also risk your job. It may be the captain's fault that the ship went aground, but the chief mate and even the third mate will bear some stigma for having been aboard. And if there is no more ship, they may face a bout of unemployment as well.

The final situation that can bring your loyalty to a justifiable, though perhaps only temporary, end occurs when your boss takes or plans to take steps that threaten you or your employees with serious and *unjustifiable* harm. The emphasis on "unjustifiable" underscores the fact that not everything a boss does that endangers an employee should be cause for combat. Progress and improvement imply change, and change customarily causes some injuries. If you or some or all of your subordinates are among those being injured, as when your own functions are being reduced or eliminated, you should think carefully before responding. If, from your boss's perspective and from the perspective of others, that step seems warranted in terms of the organization's overall good, you may be able to do yourself more good than harm by going along with it and even helping implement it. If, on the other hand, you can make a convincing case that the intended action is ill-considered, and possibly ill-motivated as well, you should think about marshaling whatever resources you can command and giving battle.

We come now to the crucial question of just how to give battle when any of these conditions occurs. Your tactics will, of course, vary from situation to situation. When an action is clearly illegal, for example, you may find it best merely to inform the appropriate authority, such as your boss's boss or even a law enforcement agency. In other instances, especially when the wrongness of an action is less clear-cut, you may wish to proceed more slowly and subtly. However, in most cases you will find the following general guidelines useful.

Document your case as fully and meticulously as you can. Keep a running record of all relevant meetings, orders, and so on and retain the originals or make copies of all relevant documents. If your boss is having lunch with someone for the purpose of arranging a kickback on an order, note carefully the time and place of the event even though you will not be present to learn exactly what is said. (Presumably you will have other data to indicate that such a kickback is being planned.)

In the process of doing this, you should try to assemble *tangible* proof of your boss's improper or unwise activity. If, for example, he tells you orally to cancel all shipments to the ABC company and you regard this decision as potentially disastrous, you can notify him in writing when you have carried it out. "As per your instruction, I have canceled all shipments to the ABC company," you can write, creating a record of what has occurred while absolving yourself of responsibility for its occurrence.

As will be evident, such a memo also places the onus for the decision squarely on the shoulders of the one who made it. This brings us to the second guideline: *Place as much distance between yourself and the wrong action as possible.* To take another example, suppose your boss has called a staff meeting to discuss a decision that you feel will have calamitous consequences. If you know your boss is determined to go through with it, you might want to look for an excuse not to attend the meeting. Cowardice? Possibly, but if the decision is already a fait accompli, your absence not only may enable you to escape some of its ill effects but may leave you in a better position to rectify it at a later date. Many a subordinate has resorted to this tactic when faced with such a situation.

Normally, however, when you find yourself diametrically opposed to your boss on a given issue, you will want to encourage meetings, and this brings us to the third guideline: *Open up the situation as much as possible.* Whenever you believe your boss is doing something wrong, whether through impropriety or through ineptness, you should exert every effort to get others involved. Thus, you should encourage establishing of interdepartmental or intradepartmental committees, calling in outside consultants or staff specialists from headquarters, and contacting of house organs, trade journals, and other media. None of this need be done with the express purpose of exposing the particular activity or decision that you have in mind. But faulty action is much more likely to be detected and deterred when committees are meeting and outsiders are coming through the door.

The fourth guideline is merely an outgrowth of a basic principle of handling people generally: *Focus your fight on the activity, not the person.* No matter how much you may have come to dislike your boss, concentrate your opposition on what he is doing or plans to do, not on him as an individual. This is not only a more honorable but also a more effective way to fight; for the more you depersonalize your case, the stronger it will seem. Moreover, if you lose the fight, you will in most instances have sustained fewer wounds and suffered fewer scars in the process.

This brings us to a final point. When, if ever, should you deliberately try to "fire" your boss? The answer is never or almost never. First of all, such moves seldom succeed. The survey of seventy-three successful executives mentioned earlier found that only six had ever attempted such a serious step, and of these, only two had succeeded. And remember, these were executives of above-average ability who eventually made it to the top. If you decide to make it a case of "it's either him or me," keep in mind that it will probably be you, not he, who is forced to leave.

Even if you do succeed in getting rid of your boss, you may find the fruits of victory to be far from what you expected. A reputation as a boss killer, like a reputation for disloyalty in general, can produce more problems than prospects for your subsequent career. Your next boss may agree that your previous one deserved his fate and yet not like you any better for having brought it about. At a minimum, your next boss is likely to hold you at arm's length lest you try to inflict the same fate on her.

Any out-and-out battle with your boss should therefore be undertaken only after careful deliberation. Once under-

---

GETTING EVEN — SOMETIMES

Although revenge is often costly and counterproductive, many a disgruntled employee has found a way to sample its questionable delights.

One such employee had a horribly bad-tempered boss who frequently and fiercely exploded at the least indication that things were not going the way he wanted. This harassed subordinate finally found a measure of satisfaction in sending his inflammable superior an anonymous get-well card after each of his blowups.

Then there was the squad of soldiers who hated their sadistic drill sergeant. Their chance came when they heard that their superior was up for promotion and that *his* superior had come to inspect his work. Taking advantage of the occasion, the soldiers proceeded to foul up every command their sergeant gave them. The promotion did not materialize.

Another group of irate employees took a different tack. When their intolerble boss landed a better job with another company, they decided to celebrate his departure with a going-away party. They publicized the party throughout the company, along with the fact that the departing boss himself had most cordially *not* been invited.

taken, it should be targeted at the particular activity or activities that prompted it. And, to the maximum extent possible, it should involve others so that if a beheading does result, the blood will not be on your hands alone. Battles with bosses are invariably difficult and dangerous, but if they are waged carefully, they can sometimes be worth the effort.

HOW CAN I GET MY BOSS TO MAKE A DECISION?

As we saw in Chapter 3, indecisive bosses are often harder to work for than the insensitive and tyrannical ones so often depicted in fiction and less often found in reality. For a subordinate can frequently learn how to get around a despot or an egoist, but handling an indecisive boss presents a whole new array of problems.

Occasionally such a boss will simply abandon his decision-making role altogether and allow you to take over. This can pose quite a dilemma if you are not prepared for the responsibility. Even if you are prepared, you may still run into trouble, for lacking his title and authority you may be unable to elicit the respect and support you need to perform his functions. In fact, your fellow employees and other managers as well may come to look upon you as a usurper and resent the role you are trying to play.

Usually, however, the indecisive manager will not hand over the reins to you or anyone else. He refuses to budge from the driver's seat—I should perhaps say buckboard to preserve the analogy—but at the same time refuses to point out the path he wishes you to follow. Or if he does point in one direction, he soon becomes overwhelmed with reservations and changes direction.

You can sometimes overcome such indecision by emphasizing and even creating deadlines. Statements such as "Sales must know this by the end of the month in order to assign the territories" or "If Production doesn't get a go-ahead by the end of the month they won't be able to order the right inventory" or "After today Smith won't have access to the main computer terminal until next Monday" may prod your boss into making up his mind.

When such stratagems fail to work, you may be able to force the issue by stating what course you want to follow and then leaving it to your boss to veto it. For instance, you might say, "ABC company seems to offer us the best deal for new typewriters. Please let me know if you feel I should not give them the order." Since voicing disapproval requires a decision on his part, and since he dislikes making decisions, you may in this fashion obtain a judgment by default. However, you should, where possible, put or confirm such statements in writing so that your fearful boss cannot later raise a fuss and claim that you acted without his authority.

Finally, if a boss fears both making a decision himself and letting you make one for him, he may not mind surrendering such responsibility to a committee. You can suggest setting up a worker-management committee to "review" various issues of general importance or several committees to work on more specific matters. This device often appeals to indecisive bosses, since delegating to one or more committees may seem less threatening to their role and position than abandoning authority to one or more individuals. In fact, they can pose as avant garde managers committed to the new, participatory work ethic. Thus their weakness can, at least in their own eyes, be made to look like strength.

HOW DO I HANDLE A BOSS
WHO IS DISPLEASED WITH ME?

First make sure that the boss really is displeased. Many employees become oversensitive to the smallest slight from their bosses and treat any gruffness of manner or failure to say good morning as a sign of imminent dismissal. Bosses are subject to as many changes of mood as anyone else. You may have been gruff to your family at breakfast that morning, but that does not mean you don't value them.

The best indicator for determining whether you have really fallen out of favor is what could be called the assignment index. If your boss is still counting on you to do things for her, then the odds are that if you have slipped in her esteem you haven't slipped very far. But if you find yourself not being given many assignments, especially of the more challenging sort, and if you are not being invited to office meetings that someone holding your position would normally be expected to attend, then there's a good chance your relationship with your superior could use some shoring up.*

Assuming that you have good reason for concluding that you are on the outs with your boss, there are various steps you can take to deal with it. The first, naturally enough, is to find out why. You can use your mentor or someone else to make the necessary inquiries, but business consultant Charles Vance recommends a more direct approach. "When you realize the boss is angry with you," he writes, "go to him/her and say 'I'm puzzled by what happened. Will you explain it to me?' *Then listen.* Control any of your emotions that stupidly urge you to get angry or protest. When the boss finishes say, 'I see the situation more clearly now. Here is what I think can be done to clear it up.'" (Fader, 1978) (The emphasis on listening, by the way, is Vance's.)

There is much to be said for such a step. Note especially the way Vance has worded the subordinate's concluding statement. In it the subordinate does not attempt to blame either the boss or himself or herself. In fact, the statement does not discuss what caused the crisis at all. Rather it focuses solely on what can be done to correct it.

Such an approach does have limitations. For one thing,

---

*Bosses, I should point out, sometimes have their own highly individualistic ways of telegraphing their displeasure. One of the more idiosyncratic was that used by Harold Ross, the founding editor of *The New Yorker*. Ross hated to fire people, so when he wanted to get rid of someone he would start removing furniture from that person's office. The employee would come to work one morning and find his clothes tree missing. A few mornings later he might find his visitor's chair or filing cabinet gone. By the time his office was stripped of everything but his desk, he would have gotten the hint and resigned.

some bosses dislike such directness and may therefore dislike you all the more if you confront them in this fashion. For another thing, you may already know why you have incurred the boss's displeasure. In such cases you may be able to use a modification of the approach and simply say that you understand why you have been displeasing her and present, or offer to discuss, ways of not doing so in the future.

There are less direct ways of handling the problem. You can, for instance, do an extra-fine job on your next assignment, or you can undertake an unassigned task that you know your boss would like to see done. If you have built up any goodwill with someone your boss respects, you may wish to ask that person to put in a discreet word in your behalf. This may work best if your advocate does not go out of his way to praise you as a person but merely mentions a specific instance or two when you have been helpful.

One tactic that can be employed to advantage, provided the problem does not go too deep, is to put some geographical distance between the two of you. If you can arrange matters so that either you or your boss will be out of the office for a while, you may find that the tension has diminished and possibly dissipated by the time the absent party returns. So this could be a good time to take your overdue vacation, military leave of absence, or field inspection trip. If your previous work has been satisfactory, your temporary absence should help clear the air.

Sometimes an appropriate absence can do more than just smooth over a temporary estrangement. It can reverse the entire direction of a deteriorating relationship.

A newly hired editor ran into trouble with her boss almost as soon as she arrived on the job. The problem was chiefly one of different views of her scope of authority, but personality differences may also have been a factor. As a way out, the editor decided to hit the road.

For the next year she was out of her office more than she was in it as she traveled around the country promoting the publishing house's books and signing up authors for new ones. Before the year was up her efforts had begun bearing fruit. Her boss was getting commendations on how well his division was doing. Both have since been promoted—she now holds his job—and although one could not call them bosom buddies, they have established a sound and mutually rewarding relationship.

HOW CAN I AVOID BEING BLAMED FOR THE SHORTCOMINGS OF FELLOW EMPLOYEES?

Anyone familiar with work organizations knows they are governed by informal codes of behavior that can be more rigidly observed, and more rigorously enforced, than their official rules. And the most pervasive and persistent of such codes is the bar against informing on a fellow employee. Bosses themselves usually respect this informal rule, and few of them will respect you for openly violating it. Reinforcing their inherent disdain of tattletales is the fact that they like to pride themselves on running a harmonious and happy operation and therefore tend to react negatively to any indication of discord in their ranks. When you point a guilty finger at another employee, you are also pointing out that such discord exists (the discord being, of course, between you and the person you are accusing).

But if squealing on a fellow employee may earn you little standing with your boss, doing nothing about the situation will hardly please him either. Bosses expect their employees to show a vital interest in and assume some responsibility for the organization's general welfare. "Doing nothing about someone else's negligence," says Paul Charlup, chairman of the board of Savin Business Machines, "is like letting a drunk get into a car or letting a two-year-old play at the end of a dock without a life jacket." (Schoenberg, 1978)

In the face of such contradictory expectations and demands, how should you deal with a co-worker whose misfeasance and nonfeasance are damaging the organization and, directly or indirectly, damaging or threatening to damage you as well?

The best, if hardly the easiest, way of handling such a situation is to persuade the offending party to stop his offensive actions. And the argument most likely to accomplish this is one that appeals to his self-interest. If you can find a good reason that he will do himself some good, or spare himself some harm, by doing as you suggest, you will in most instances have taken a giant step toward solving the problem. And if you can also convince him that one of your motives in bringing it to his attention is concern for *his* welfare, so much the better.

A schoolteacher became greatly upset when she learned that a fellow teacher was disciplining her pupils by smacking them on the hand with a ruler. This practice greatly offended the first teacher's sense of how schoolchildren should be treated. It was also against their state's law. The latter fact provided the concerned teacher with a means of getting her colleague to stop. She pointed out to the ruler-wielding teacher the danger she ran in administering such punishment, adding that it would be a shame to have anything like this disrupt her career. She also pointed out that such disciplinary methods could cause great trouble for their school principal, a man whom they both liked. The hand smacking soon stopped.

If you cannot make use of such a technique in a given situation, then you can often call the problem to your boss's attention without singling out a particular offender. In the above situation, for example, the upset teacher could have told the principal, "I think that some faculty members don't fully understand the law barring corporal punishment. It might be helpful if you put out a memo clarifying it." She might then have shown him a draft of a memo that she had prepared on the subject. Whether or not the principal issued the memo and whether or not it accomplished its purpose, she would have alerted him to the existence of the problem and possibly prompted him to probe a bit further on his own.

Sometimes you can ask your boss to look into a situation without necessarily identifying the problem, let alone the person or persons responsible for it. If, for example, some members of your work group refuse to carry their share of the load, you can suggest a productivity study. As a general rule, you may find it more effective to refrain from directly exposing an unsavory situation yourself and instead to stimulate initiatives that will automatically lead to its exposure.

At times your boss may bluntly ask for your opinion about a fellow employee. If you harbor reservations about the individual, try to convey them to your boss in as tactful and as positive a way as possible. For a secretary who would rather talk than type, you can say, "He's a pleasant, outgoing person, but I wonder if he wouldn't be happier serving as a receptionist or in some other position that would allow him more chances to interact with people." For a well-groomed salesperson who quits too early, "She makes a nice appearance and I'm sure she impresses the customers. However, you might want to compare her sales figures with those of our other new salespeople." (Of course, this won't necessarily reveal her early quitting time, but if she maintains a decent sales record, why should you or your boss care when she leaves for home?) For a new computer programmer who lacks some essential skills, you might say, "He programs fairly well in BASIC, but he might benefit from some further training in other computer languages."

There may be times when such approaches will not suffice. A situation may arise that is so serious or sensitive that you must act forcefully and immediately. If this should also require you to implicate a fellow employee, then there is a way to do so without necessarily making yourself a squealer.

The method, though quite simple, can also be quite unpleasant to execute. It requires you to inform the offending co-worker of your intention to tell the boss about his offenses and then invite him to be present to defend himself. Taking such a step may give you a reputation for having too much company loyalty and for playing hardball. But it will also demonstrate that you do not knife someone in the back and that you take your job and your organization's mission seriously.*

Having said all this, I should point out that you should ignore most of the peccadillos of your fellow employees. Even when their misbehavior or nonbehavior affects your job, if the damage is only slight and occasional, your best course of action may be to forget about it. Nearly all of us are blamed occasionally for things that are not our fault, and often the wisest thing we can do is to do nothing. Work, like most other areas of life, spawns all kinds of wrongs that we would like to right. Success, however, lies in trying to change only those wrongs that really matter and that lend themselves to rectification, while going along with the rest.

MY BOSS GIVES ME MORE WORK
THAN I CAN POSSIBLY HANDLE

Congratulations! A boss who overloads you with work is one who values your work. If she hasn't given you much consideration as a person, she has at least shown a lot of consideration for you as a performer. A boss who's piling the work on you is not likely to be thinking of replacing you.

Nonetheless, the situation is aggravating, exhausting, and ultimately perilous. If you say nothing but merely struggle on, your boss, hearing no complaint, will be tempted to load more and more work on you. Then, as you start to fall behind, she will become annoyed, for in accepting more as-

---

*In the famous "trial" of J. Robert Oppenheimer in 1954, the government, in an effort to strip the father of the atomic bomb of his security clearance, called the noted scientist Edward Teller to testify. Realizing that what he said would hurt Oppenheimer, whose policies he detested, Teller stipulated that he would testify only in Oppenheimer's presence. Though Teller's testimony damaged his relationship with the scientific community, which generally supported Oppenheimer, his insistence that his fellow scientist be present when he spoke against him preserved his reputation as well as his self-respect.

signments than you can handle, you have implicitly made promises you cannot fulfill.

You must, therefore, bring the matter to her attention. But rather than confront her with a complaint, try a more positive tack. Point out that you want to make sure you are giving priority to what she regards as most important, so ask her to list or clarify her priorities so that you can follow them in discharging your duties.

This approach should in most cases permit you to point out the problem to your boss without having to carp or complain. In fact, it reaffirms your loyalty and willingness to serve, for it shows you are concerned with trying to meet her needs.

If your boss fails to get the hint, you may have to become more forthright and specific. If, for example, she gives you one assignment and then immediately adds another, ask her which one she considers to have the higher priority and proceed from there. If you fail to execute the one of lesser importance, then at least you know that it was the less important one, and at least your boss knows that you bothered to find out beforehand. Eventually she should become aware of the situation and, assuming that the fault is hers and not yours in being too slow or inefficient, should take some steps to correct it.

HOW CAN I GET MY BOSS
TO GIVE ME A RAISE OR PROMOTION?

Many boss problems, like so many health, crime, and other problems, are best dealt with through prevention. The classic employee dilemma of how to obtain a raise or a promotion offers a good example of what I mean. This delicate and often difficult question can frequently be averted through proper planning and foresight.

Instead of asking for each raise or promotion, you should, at the time you come on the job or as soon thereafter as practicable, ask your boss for a career plan. Such a plan should include a schedule for moving ahead, based, of course, on the assumption that your work is satisfactory. If you can persuade your boss to work out such a plan, or to approve one that you submit, you may never have to request a raise or promotion. All you will have to do is to remind the boss when it comes time to implement the plan's next step.

Although the career-plan approach generally provides the most satisfactory solution to the raise-or-promotion problem, it may not work in every specific situation. Your boss may dislike committing herself in such a fashion, your organization's future may be too uncertain to permit it, or you may believe you can fare better with a more flexible arrangement. Moreover, some bosses, even when they have agreed to such a plan, become quite lethargic when it comes to implementing it. Such behavior can defeat much of the plan's purpose, since it forces you to specifically request each of its stipulated steps.

If you find yourself without a career plan or with a career plan that your boss seems to have forgotten about, here are a few suggestions that may help you obtain the raise or promotion you believe to be your due.

Give your boss some advance notice. Before actually broaching the subject with your boss, drop a hint or two that it is on your mind. In this way you will not catch her unprepared when it comes time to discuss it. You may think this will only give her a chance to fabricate reasons to reject your request, but remember that your goal is not to win an argument. It is to convince your boss that bestowing the sought-for benefit is in the interests of all concerned. If your boss has any reservations, you should want to know about them. (You may find, after hearing them, that you're in the wrong job or with the wrong company.)

Pick an appropriate time. Ordinarily, this will be when your boss is in a good mood, and if her euphoria has been caused or catalyzed by something you did, so much the better. Time of day can also matter. Confronting your boss with your demand the first thing in the morning will rarely prove advantageous. As noted in Chapter 3, people, and especially managers, are usually more relaxed in the afternoon. But don't wait until five minutes to five before bringing up the subject unless certain circumstances seem to make it a propitious moment.

Document your accomplishments. Instead of telling your boss how hard you have worked, show her what you have actually done. Try to develop some concrete measures using numbers, especially percentages, to demonstrate this. You can also cite specific examples of achievements if appropriate ones exist. Avoid descriptive adjectives and adverbs. Don't say, for instance, "I landed a big order with the ABC company," but rather "I landed a $40,000 order with the ABC company." In other words, let the facts speak for themselves as much as possible.

Carrying this last point a bit further, you may find it best to *say* nothing about your work and instead simply to hand your boss a one-page statement summarizing what you have done. In this way she will have in black and white an itemized list of your accomplishments that she can read quickly and later refer to. At the same time, you will be spared having to say things that will inevitably sound boastful and self-serving.

Point out any benefits to your boss. Admittedly, this is not always easy to do, for you are the one who is asking for something, and your boss is the one who, out of resources that may be limited, must decide whether to grant your request. Still, if you look hard enough, you may come up with some reasons that the requested raise or promotion can prove beneficial to the grantor as well as to the grantee.

If you are seeking a promotion, you can point out how the increased authority will enable you to do more things for your boss or enable you to do the things you now do more expeditiously. If you are seeking a raise, you can, if nothing else, mention that it will show others that satisfactory work is rewarded. Making a compelling or even convincing case that your boss will appreciably advance her own interests in advancing yours may take a bit of thinking on your part, but more often than not it will be worth the effort.

Don't threaten. Bosses tend to bristle when subordinates threaten to resign or to go over their heads if a demand is not met. Even when the boss yields to the threat, the superior–subordinate relationship loses a measure of trust that will be difficult if not impossible to recapture. Under such conditions a momentary victory can turn into a long-term loss. On the other hand, if your boss turns you down but seems to have a good reason for doing so, you may do yourself a lot of good by assuring her of your continued effort and support. This may well prompt her to go out of her way to redress the situation as soon as she can. And a stronger link between the two of you will have been forged.

I DO MY JOB SO WELL THAT MY BOSS WON'T LET ME DO ANYTHING ELSE

This has happened to more than one able subordinate. Although you can normally expect excellent performance to open up new opportunities, sometimes it does the opposite. Your boss may come to depend so heavily on you to do the things that you have been doing well that he refuses to let you do anything else. As a result, your skills remain underdeveloped, and your career stagnates.

When this happens, you must look for ways to break out of the rut. There are two occasions when such opportunities are most likely to occur: slack times and emergencies.

Regarding the first, nearly all positions have periods when their activity eases up. You should take advantage of such times to undertake something beyond your normal routine. If, for example, your job requires you to compile data for others to write up, you might suggest that you try doing some of the writing as well. Or if your job consists of selling item A but not item B, you might ask for a chance to see what you can do with item B.

Your desire to transcend your normal scope of activity need not take the form of actually *doing* something else. It can be limited to merely looking into or learning about something else. If you are involved in production, for instance, you might ask to spend a day or two traveling with a salesperson or helping out in finance. Whatever form your request takes, it will give your boss a clear signal that you want to expand your horizons. Later on you can look for ways to put your new experience or knowledge to work through a change or enlargement of your customary duties.

If you feel your job has no slack times, you should try to create them. Possibly through organizing your work more carefully or delegating some of its functions to others, you can find some spare moments. All too often we get overcome by the day-to-day routine because we have not paused long enough and thought hard enough to discover ways of making it more manageable. Don't let this happen to you.

Then there are emergencies. Virtually every organization, no matter how stable and sedate its operations, will from time to time confront a crisis of one kind or another. Such occurrences can open up avenues for you to show what you can do. Sometimes you may be able to anticipate them by keeping yourself well informed about what is going on both inside and outside your organization. But, in any case, don't let the crisis slip through your fingers if you want a chance to demonstrate your capabilities. Not only are you more likely to get such a chance, but your efforts, if successful, are more likely to be appreciated. As a result, the next crisis, when it comes, may find you already exercising broadened responsibilities.

MY BOSS DOESN'T GIVE ME ENOUGH TO DO

This is a more pervasive problem than one might suppose. It tends to occur most often in highly professional and technical organizations, since scientists, engineers, architects, editors, professors, and other specialists frequently dislike delegating, or do not know how to delegate, meaningful responsibilities. The authors of *The Managerial Woman* indicate that many women managers also have this problem, although this may be changing rapidly as women become more familiar with managerial roles.

If fate has given you a boss who likes to hog all the work for himself, then by all means capitalize on the situation. Use the time available to improve your skills or develop new ones. Learn more about the organization, and make connections with its various segments. And, remembering that managerial work is open-ended, look for things you can do to supplement and support your boss's regular activities. For example, you can offer to prepare a report on how other companies in your field are handling a particular problem, conduct an in-house survey on how your fellow workers feel about a particular matter or group of matters, or check out a new computer system. Your boss may possibly regard any or all of your proposed projects as unnecessary or as encroaching on his own turf, but if you know him well enough, you should be able to come up with tasks that he would like to have done.

Under certain circumstances you can even propose that he loan you out on a part-time basis to some other manager whose goodwill he might like to cultivate. This in turn will give you an opportunity to learn from, and impress yourself upon, another important member of your organization. A boss who likes to do it all himself can, when well managed, become an undisguised blessing.

HOW SHOULD I HANDLE A NEW BOSS?

Your old boss leaves, and a new one takes his place. Such an event, while common enough in the world of work, can still be disquieting. Your old boss may have been far from ideal. You may have disliked and even despised him. But at least you had got to know his faults and flaws and had probably developed some techniques for dealing with them. The new boss is an unknown, and the unknown is always a bit unsettling. No matter what your relations were with your old boss, how can you be sure they won't be worse with the new one?

While there is no guaranteeing that this won't cocur, there are some easy-to-execute precautionary steps you can take to minimize such a possibility. Don't be deceived by their simplicity, for they can be surprisingly effective.

The first and by now the most obvious step is to learn as much as you can about your new superior. Since this step was discussed at length in Chapter 2, it requires no further elaboration here.

The second step is to prepare a one-page résumé and hand it to your new superior when she arrives on the job. You can make use of whatever knowledge you have acquired about her in drawing up this brief statement about yourself. If she comes from the Midwest, or graduated from an Ivy League college, or likes to play tennis, then, if you share any of these attributes, you can include them. (It might seem that a love of tennis does not belong on a document of this kind, but a line at the bottom of the page mentioning hobbies or outside interests is a legitimate résumé item.)

You may also want to prepare a second one-page statement giving a description of your job and its duties. If it is appropriate, you can describe the projects you are currently working on and where you are on them. In drawing up your job description you may wish to put first or otherwise give prominence to those functions that you prefer to do or feel that you do best. (In most cases, they will be the same ones.) By underscoring them in this fashion you can influence your new boss to think of you when it comes to assigning such duties and to give them more weight when she evaluates your overall contribution.

You will naturally offer to help your new superior to familiarize herself with the operation she now manages. At the same time, don't be too eager to do so, and don't be too disappointed if your offer is not fully accepted. New bosses frequently like to find out things for themselves, and they may shy away from subordinates who seem too zealous to "show them the ropes."

Finally, don't run down your old boss no matter how much you may have abominated him. Doing so will rarely endear you to your new boss, and it may make her wonder whether someday you will treat her in the same manner. In the same vein, don't retail any gossip or rumors. If there are problems that she should know about, you can suggest areas that she might wish to look into. But don't pursue the subject unless she presses you for more information.

To sum up, you should demonstrate a desire to assist your new boss while scrupulously avoiding any appearance of trying to influence her. A new boss usually appreciates assistance but is also concerned with establishing her role and authority. If you can strike a careful balance between being disinterested and being directive, between seeking to cooperate and seeking to control, you can lay the foundation for an excellent superior–subordinate relationship.

IN CONCLUSION: THREE CAUTIONS

6

It is to be hoped that this exploratory foray into what might be called the underside of management will equip and encourage you to move a bit further and faster along in your career. But even if it achieves this modest goal, it will certainly provide no panaceas. As noted earlier, human relationships of any kind are far too complex to permit anyone to put forth a set of ready-made responses for all the challenges that these relationships continually present. And this may be especially true when it comes to the shadowy area of boss management.

These reflections bring us to the first cautionary comment: Don't treat any of the points raised or suggestions set forth in the preceding chapters as an inflexible rule to be observed on all occasions and at all costs. Although some of them might seem worth adhering to in all situations—the admonitions about listening, for example—there may well be times when they too should be put aside. The subject simply does not lend itself to prefabricated prescriptions that can be universally applied.

But, you may now be thinking, if I am not to take all that has been said as inevitably and invariably binding, then why should I work so hard to try to implement it? This brings us to the second cautionary comment, which is that you really should not work too hard at trying to manage your boss. Indeed, doing so can be self-defeating.

To see why this is so, let us look at one of the basic laws of economics, the law of diminishing returns. It tells us that putting more and more resources, be they money, manpower, muscle, or what have you, into any undertaking will eventually produce less and less additional output. Eventually a point will be reached where such additional investments will actually lead to reduced outputs.

This law applies to human investments as well. Too great an expenditure of effort can sometimes yield less of a return than a more modest outlay. Thus, the lover who pursues his love object with zeal frequently overplays his hand and ends up a loser. The same can be true of the subordinate who takes the task of handling his boss too seriously. Boss management requires a measure of cool objectivity that only detachment can supply. Too great a concentration on the process can easily prove self-defeating.

There is another, more palpable reason why too much time and effort expended on handling your boss can prove dysfunctional and damaging. It can distract you from giving the proper attention to your own work; and while good performance alone may not be sufficient to achieve your career goals (see Chapter 1), it certainly has an important and often indispensable role to play. A career built on boss management alone can eventually crumble, for sooner or later the lack of real substance, that is, of true accomplishment, will show through.

One of the most skillful boss managers I have ever met was a political science professor at a large eastern university. He so impressed his superiors that he managed to become chairman of his department, then dean of his college, and then primary nominee for university provost. Still in his thirties, he seemed a sure bet to become the university's next president. But while he was adeptly handling his superiors, he was mismanaging his own responsibilities and alienating his subordinates. Consequently, when the university submitted his nomination for provost to the faculty senate, it was roundly rejected. With his remarkable and seemingly relentless rise to the top abruptly ended, he felt compelled to resign and take an administrative position with a southern university, where, at last report, he was experiencing similar difficulties.

To put the second cautionary comment in capsule form: Don't overdo. Keep your relationship with your boss in good running order, but don't let it become the overriding issue in your work life. Above all, don't let it interfere with your real work.

One step that may help you maintain the proper perspective is not to want or need your job too much. If you look on your job as the sine qua non of your career, you may become too concerned with your superior's opinion of you, and this can lead to a lot of counterproductive behavior on your part. If, on the other hand, you have planned one or more alternative courses of action you could pursue should you ever lose your job, then you may be able to handle both the job and your boss more effectively. Having such fall-back courses of action in mind may help you avoid the missteps that a feeling of insecurity can so easily foster. The knowledge that all will not be lost should you and your superior reach an impasse may well prevent such an impasse from ever developing.

The third and final cautionary comment may seem almost contradictory to everything that has been said: Don't try to manipulate your boss, or at least don't try to manipulate him too much. To put it another way, stay honest and aboveboard.

Of course, we all continually engage in manipulation in the sense that we use various techniques in dealing with people. In this sense, psychotherapists manipulate when they use indirect and subtle methods to induce their patients to confront problems that the latter would rather not recognize. And parents can be said to manipulate their children when they read the books psychologists write and seek to put their suggestions into effect. Yet most of us would hesitate to label such tactics outright manipulation, since they do not seem inherently deceitful. Rather, their aim is to help those toward whom they are directed achieve their own essential goals and realize their own potentialities.

Boss management in most cases should be no different. Managing superiors, like managing subordinates, is not inherently a zero-sum game. One party's gain does not necessitate the other party's loss. On the contrary, the interests of the two tend to converge. Good boss management should help both you and your boss do a better job, generating in the process blessings and benefits for all concerned.

APPENDIX:
MANAGING
MULTIPLE BOSSES

Although traditional management books generally stress the undesirability of serving two or more masters, many managers have long had to work under such conditions. Examples are corporation presidents who report to boards of directors, city managers who answer to city councils, and executive secretaries who seek to carry out the wishes of their commissions or committees.

In recent years, still more varieties of multiple bosses have appeared on the scene. The ever-growing insistence on increased democracy and participation in organizational life has led to a proliferation of worker–management, clientele, and other kinds of committees. And while such groups can seldom dictate decisions to the manager with whom they deal, they can exert much influence on his or her actions. They thus become, in a sense, quasi bosses whose orders need not always be accepted but whose wishes can never be completely disregarded.

In dealing with multiple bosses, you can make use of many of the same techniques and tactics you would employ in handling single superiors. To begin with, you should learn as much as you can about them. Obviously you cannot expect to learn as much about each individual member of the group as you would expect to find out about a single, immediate superior. Obtaining such information not only would take too much time but also would require more opportunity to work with them than you are likely to have. Nevertheless, if your multiple-boss group is of manageable size, you should try to assemble some basic data about each member.

Since you are now dealing with several individuals, you may find it helpful to maintain actual files on each one, adding items of interest to each dossier as they come your way. For example, although the record of each meeting will show how they all voted on the issues that came before them, you may wish to go a step further and record each member's vote on each issue in the member's own file. Such record keeping can have many uses, for it gives you a profile of the member's voting patterns and thereby some indication of how this member may vote in the future.

Your files need not and should not be limited to actions taken at meetings of the group. How the members reacted to other matters that were discussed, and how they react to each other, are matters of likely interest and import. Nor should personal data be overlooked. If you know that one key member is a proud alumna of a particular college, you might wish to consider this in choosing college interns. If you know that another member loves to fish, you may want to keep this in mind in choosing a site for a weekend conference. And if a meeting falls on a member's birthday, you may wish to make an appropriate gesture or remark.

In nearly all groups, some members tend to assume a more dominant role than others. You will therefore tend to treat them with extra consideration and care. This is only natural and to some extent wise—but only to some extent.

Never neglect the more subdued and self-effacing of your multiple bosses, for if ignored they can fall under the influence of the more dominant ones, thereby making the latter more powerful and less manageable. Unless your group is unusually structured or has unusual procedures, the votes of the weak will count as much as those of the strong. Try to ensure that they will more often than not be on your side.

In handling the leaders of your group, you will usually find it in your interest to allow and even encourage them to exercise the more symbolic aspects of leadership, such as representing the group at various functions and serving as spokespersons to the news media. If, for example, some reporters call with urgent requests for information on a particular matter, refer them to the group chairperson or to the chairperson of the group's appropriate subcommittee. You may then add that if the person you designate is unavailable, the reporters can call you back and you will try to accommodate them. If the matter is complex or controversial, you might say that you will have an appropriate person call them back. You can then try to reach the person or persons you have in mind and brief them before they speak to the media representatives.

To continue with this example, suppose that no appropriate member or members of your multiple-boss group are available, or that if any are available they would be too biased or bombastic in what they said to let them talk with the press. You will then try to supply the information yourself. But as soon as you have done so, you should think immediately about informing the leaders, and possibly all the members, of your multiple-boss team. For they will understandably find it annoying and embarrassing to have to learn what's going on within their group through an outside source such as a newspaper or newscast.

This brings us to another essential of multiple-boss management: Keep your bosses informed. Send them copies of press releases, important correspondence, and other materials that will let them know what you are doing. At times you may hesitate because you fear hostile reactions from one or more recalcitrant members, but in most instances you will incur less displeasure and dissent if you keep the lines of communication open.

As in individual boss management, you can sometimes limit the effect of a potentially damaging development by divulging it yourself. An incident involving a liberal school superintendent and the most conservative member of his school committee offers a good illustration of this technique.

An aide walked into the superintendent's office one afternoon and showed him a nearly obscene cartoon in the just-printed high school student newspaper. Knowing that the outspokenly conservative committeeman would soon learn of the cartoon, make a big issue of it at the committee meeting, and probably hold him responsible, the superintendent decided to act. He immediately called the committeeman at his law office and asked if he could come to see him. On arriving, the superintendent displayed the cartoon, threw up his hands in dismay, and asked the committee member what he thought they should do about it. In this fashion he not only deflected the member's potential wrath away from himself but actually converted him temporarily into an ally.

In many cases you will have some intimation of an impending unpleasant development. When you do, it is usually wise to drop a hint or two that it is coming. If you are a sales manager and reports from the field indicate that sales for the quarter are likely to show a falloff, you can mention to your board or committee how fussy your customers have become. If you are a city manager faced with reporting a severe cost overrun on a construction project, you can mention ahead of time how the weather is playing havoc with the construction schedule. At times it may be advantageous to spring the bad news out of the blue, but more often some preparation is advisable.

In revealing bad news to multiple bosses, you should, as you would with a single boss, try at the same time to present some good news or some alternative courses of action. I recall a time when I served on the board of directors of a small company that had developed a new machine for cleaning computer tapes. We had persuaded a major corporation to market it for us and were eagerly anticipating the handsome profits that would ensue when suddenly we learned that the corporation had decided to drop the device. We were certainly a disconsolate bunch of would-be entrepreneurs when we showed up at a hastily scheduled meeting in our president's office to discuss this dire development. But our clever president had quickly assembled an impressive display of other products he was working on. While his show did not completely succeed in turning our despair into elation, we did come away from the meeting feeling that all was not yet lost.

While multiple-boss managers usually find some of their bosses (or quasi bosses) easier to manage than others, they frequently learn that even the most tractable members of the group can become quite intractable when a particular issue or occasion arises. You should therefore seek to establish a safe working majority with a comfortable margin left over. With this technique, you will be able to lose a supporter or two on any given issue and still prevail.

At the same time, however, you should try almost at all costs to avoid permanently alienating any member of the group. There are nearly always some matters on which you and all the members can agree, and you should provide opportunities for such unanimity to be expressed. In arranging your agendas, try to include some items on which all of you can agree.

When it comes to presenting an important issue that is certain to arouse the antagonism of one or more members, you should make doubly sure that your relations with the other members are on a firm footing. As one boss manager who reported to a three-member board once remarked, "Whenever I fight with one of them, I make damn sure I am getting along well with the other two." In organizational combat, as in military combat, it is poor practice to fight on two fronts at the same time.

There is another basic rule of organizational combat you should observe even more rigorously when you lock horns with one or more of your multiple bosses. This rule is to win without laughing and lose without crying. When you win, never gloat or display even the slightest sign of triumphant delight. Instead, move as expeditiously as possible to reduce your opponents' rancor. Salve their bruised egos by conceding a point of lesser importance or, at a minimum, promising to keep their reservations about the issue in mind. When victory goes the other way, you should not treat the outcome as a crushing personal defeat. Instead, show yourself ready to make the best of it (unless, of course, it involves considerations so crucial as to mandate your resignation).

Given the problems and perils that pushing through a controversial matter may entail, many multiple-boss managers look for others to shoulder as much of the burden as possible. Generally, they seek out the more effective among those members whose support they can rely on and then arm them with facts, figures, arguments, and sometimes even strategies that they can use. They may also suggest calling in outside experts, setting up special study committees, or developing new or improved management information systems when they feel they can count on such devices to support their side. And usually they will have prepared fallback positions they can retreat to, that is, alternatives that will allow them to gain at least some part of what they seek.

More aggressive managers have often exercised a measure of control over the membership of the group itself. Nearly all groups experience some turnover, and these alert managers always have a list of potential replacements to recommend when this occurs. Since the other members will probably have given little thought to the problem, such managers can often make their recommendations prevail.

Finally, there is one further tactic that is more openly manipulative. This tactic is to bombard the members with information. Proposals are incorporated into voluminous reports or other lengthy documents that no member of the group will have time to read. Reluctant to confess that they are intimidated by so much data, all or most of the group may quietly go along with whatever the report recommends. This technique is a great favorite with many school superintendents who use it to get school committees to approve what they want to do. But as with most deliberately manipulative devices, this one can backfire. The members may become increasingly irritated over having to sanction policies and projects that they have had no real opportunity to examine and think through for themselves, and their irritation may find other avenues of expression. So if school superintendents frequently enjoy great success in getting school committees to ratify their recommendations, it should also be noted that their profession tends to suffer from a high turnover rate as well. With multiple bosses as with single bosses, an essentially honest approach works best for all concerned.

BIBLIOGRAPHY

ADAMS, HENRY H. *Harry Hopkins.* New York: G. P. Putnam's Sons, 1977.

ARGYRIS, CHRIS. *Organization and Innovation.* New Haven: Yale University Press, 1963.

BEVERIDGE, ALBERT J. *Abraham Lincoln.* Boston: Houghton Mifflin Company, 1982.

BRZEZINSKI, ZBIGNIEW. *Power and Principle.* New York: Farrar, Straus & Giroux, 1983.

CARNEGIE, ANDREW. *Autobiography.* Boston: Houghton Mifflin Company, 1920.

CARO, ROBERT A. *The Power Broker: Robert Moses and the Fall of New York.* New York: Vintage Books, 1975.

CHESTERTON, G. K. *Heretics.* London: John Lane, 1904.

CROSBY, PHILIP B. *The Art of Getting Your Own Sweet Way.* New York: McGraw-Hill, 1982.

DELANEY, WILLIAM A. *The Thirty Most Common Problems in Management and How to Solve Them.* New York: American Management Association, 1982.

DRUCKER, PETER, F. *The Practice of Management.* New York: Harper & Row, 1954.

EHRLICHMAN, JOHN. *Witness to Power: The Nixon Years.* New York: Simon & Schuster, 1982.

EISENHOWER, DWIGHT D. *At Ease.* Garden City, N.Y.: Doubleday & Co., 1967.

FADER, SHIRLEY SLOAN (pseud. S. R. Redford). *Jobmanship.* New York: Macmillan, 1978.

FRANKEL, CHARLES. *High on Foggy Bottom.* New York: Harper & Row, 1968.

GINOTT, HIAM G. *Between Parent and Child.* New York: Macmillan, 1965.

GOLD, KENNETH A. "Managing for Success: A Comparison of the Private and Public Sectors." *Public Administration Review,* November/December 1982.

HALBERSTAM, DAVID. *The Best and the Brightest.* New York: Random House, 1969.

HASLIP, JOAN. *Catherine the Great: A Biography.* New York: G. P. Putnam's Sons, 1977.

HENNIG, MARGARET, and JARDIN, ANNE. *The Managerial Woman.* Garden City, N.Y.: Doubleday & Co., 1976.

KATZ, DANIEL, and KAHN, ROBERT L. *The Social Psychology of Organizations.* New York: John Wiley & Sons, 1966.

KOTTER, JOHN P. *The General Manager.* New York: The Free Press, 1982.

LOMBARDO, MICHAEL M., and MCCALL, MORGAN W., JR. "The Intolerable Boss." *Psychology Today,* January 1984.

LONGFORD, ELIZABETH. *Wellington: The Years of the Sword.* New York: Harper & Row, 1969.

MCFEELY, WILLIAM S. *Grant.* New York: W. W. Norton & Co., 1981.

MCGREGOR, DOUGLAS. *The Theory of Human Enterprise.* New York: McGraw-Hill, 1960.

MITCHELL, BROADUS. *Alexander Hamilton: A Concise Biography.* New York: Oxford University Press, 1976.

O'CONNELL, D. P. *Richelieu.* Cleveland: World Publishing Co., 1968.

PLOWDEN, ALISON. *Elizabeth Regina.* New York: Times Books, 1980.

SCHOENBERG, ROBERT J. *The Art of Being a Boss.* Philadelphia: J. B. Lippincott, 1978. Copyright © 1978 by Robert J. Schoenberg. Excerpts reprinted by permission of Harper & Row, Publishers, Inc., and Don Congdon Associates, Inc.

SHERWOOD, ROBERT E. *Roosevelt and Hopkins.* New York: Harper & Row, 1948.

SLOAN, ALFRED P., JR. *My Years with General Motors.* Garden City, N.Y.: Doubleday & Co., 1964.

SPEER, ALBERT. *Inside the Third Reich.* New York: Macmillan, 1970.

STEWART, ROSEMARY. *The Reality of Organizations.* New York: Anchor Books, 1972.

TAYLOR, HENRY. *The Statesman.* 1836. New York: New American Library, 1958.

TOLAND, JOHN. *Adolf Hitler.* Garden City, N.Y.: Doubleday & Co., 1976.

WALTERS, BARBARA. *How to Talk with Practically Anybody about Practically Anything.* Garden City, N.Y.: Doubleday & Co., 1983.

WILLIAMS, T. HARRY. *Lincoln and His Generals.* New York: Vintage Books, 1952.

INDEX

A

Absence, from displeased boss, 109-10
Accountability, written communication
    and, 51
Action:
    active listening and, 47-48
    postponed, 47-48
Active listening, 44-48
    action and, 47-48
    cues and, 47
    displeased boss and, 108
    emotional response and, 71
    insecurity and, 45-46
    note-taking and, 46
Age of boss, selection process and, 31-33
    See also Older bosses; Older women
Alternatives. *See* Options

Appreciation, boss selection and, 27-28
Argyris, Chris, 93
Art of Getting Your Own Sweet Way, The
    (Crosby), 95
Assignment index, displeasure of boss
    and, 108
Auchincloss, Louis, 79*n*

B

Baby boom generation, decreasing supply
    of managerial jobs for, 5
Bacon, Francis, 39, 95
Bad boss, 84-86
    getting rid of, 104-6
    revenge against, 105
    tolerating, 90
    See also Problems with boss

145

Credit, allowing boss to take, 68
Crisis:
  multiple bosses and, 134–35
  response to, 73
  See also Bad news
Criticism:
  of boss, 100–101
  suggestions and, 63
Crosby, Gordon, 49, 60
Crosby, Philip B., 95
Cues, active listening and, 47

D

Daughter, as boss, 32
Decisiveness of superior, boss selection
  and, 21–23
Delaney, William, 76
Delegating responsibility, dislike of taking
  risks and, 22
Dichter, Dr. Ernest, 72
Dickens, Charles, 82n
Discharge. *See* Dismissal
Disciplinary actions, 7
Disloyalty, 82–84
Dismissal, 6–7, 108n
  attitude toward, 127–28
  of boss, 104–6
  disloyalty and, 82
  reasons for, 9
Displeased boss, handling of, 107–10
Drucker, Peter, 3–4, 5, 6, 13
Du Pont, Pierre S., 10–11, 25

E

Educational background of boss, 40
Ego problems, of boss, 97
Ehrlichman, John, 47–48
Eisenhower, Dwight D., 8, 51, 73, 75, 81–
  82
Elements of Style, The (Strunk, Jr., and
  White), 51
Elevator speech, 49
Eliot, Frederick, 26
Elizabeth, Queen, 14, 23
Emergencies:
  expansion of skills during, 117–18
  suggestions made during, 64n
Escoffier, 28
Ethics, defense of bad policy and, 100–101
Experts, as managers, 28–30

F

Fearfulness. *See* Indecisiveness
Firings. *See* Dismissals
Flattery, 70–71
Flexibility, of boss management, 125–26
Ford, Gerald, 66
Frankel, Charles, 6

Friendship:
  with boss, 77–79
  mentoring and, 80–81
*Future of Education in New Zealand,
  The,* 69

G

Garretson, Robert, 64–65, 68, 75, 101
General Manager, The (Kotter), 9
George III, King, 97n
Ginott, Haim, 70
Gladstone, William, 33n
Goals and objectives of boss, 40
  boss selection and, 23–24
Godolphin, Sidney, 79
Gold, Kenneth A., 13
Good news, bad news along with, 93
Good performance, conditions for recog-
  nition of, 8–9
Government:
  role of management in, 4
  role of written communication in, 51
Grant, Ulysses S., 14n–15n, 61, 79n, 84
Graphs, 52–53, 56

H

Hamilton, Alexander, 44, 51
Health, boss management and, 10
Heifetz, Jascha, 29
Hennig, Margaret, 20n
History, role of subordinates in, 14–15
Hitler, Adolf, 8, 34, 46, 78, 96
Hopkins, Harry, 8, 14, 25, 47, 73, 81, 100
Hours, of arrival and departure, 76–77
Howe, Louis, 31
Humanistic ethos, relationships and, 7
Human relations practices:
  listening and, 44–45
  superior-subordinate relationships and,
    12–13
Humphrey, Hubert, 35n

I

Ideas:
  accepted, 97
  anticipating objections to, 96
  bosses' egos and, 97
  overselling, 96–97
  presenting to boss, 94–97
  presenting to multiple bosses, 135–36
  putting in writing, 94–95
  See also Bad ideas; Suggestions
Illegal acts by boss, 100, 101–6
Image of boss, improving, 67–69
Imitation, as flattery, 72–73
Immoral acts by boss, 100, 101–6
Impulsive acts, indecisiveness and, 22
Indecisive boss, 106–7
  boss selection and, 21–23